the new york times

GERSHWIN years in song

Introduction by EDWARD JABLONSKI and LAWRENCE D STEWART

Quadrangle | The New York Times Book Co.

*With elephantine thanks to **Edward Jablonski** — who brought ineffable pleasure and spirit (as well as charming photographs) with him whenever he worked on this book — and **Lawrence D. Stewart** — whose contributions were incalculable. Also to **Irving Brown,** without whom this book would not have been possible and **Norman Weiser,** President of Chappell & Co., Inc.*

For information, address: Quadrangle/The New York Times Book Co., 10 East 53rd Street, New York, New York 10022.
Manufactured in the United States of America. Published simultaneously in Canada by Fitzhenry & Whiteside, Ltd., Toronto.

Library of Congress Catalog Card Number: 73-82478
International Standard Book Number: 0-8129-0368-4

Photo Credits

Photos courtesy of Edward Jablonski, Lawrence D. Stewart, and The New York Times. Record album covers courtesy of Columbia Records, Klavier Records and Monmouth-Evergreen Records.

*Music Typography: **Music Art Co.***
*Music Proofreader: **Frank Metis***
*Jacket Design: **Jerry Lieberman***
*Book Design: **Lee Snider/Jerry Lieberman***

Jacket illustration courtesy of the artist — from the collection of Edith and Edward Jablonski

CONTENTS

Introduction	1
The Real American Folk Song (Is A Rag) (1918)	3
Swanee (1919)	9
Mischa, Yascha, Toscha, Sascha (1919)	15
I'll Build A Stairway To Paradise (1922)	19
Somebody Loves Me (1924)	23
Fascinating Rhythm (1924)	27
Oh, Lady Be Good (1924)	33
The Man I Love (1924)	36
Rhapsody In Blue (1924)	41
Looking For A Boy (1925)	43
That Certain Feeling (1925)	47
Sweet And Low-Down (1925)	51
Concerto In F (1925)	56
Maybe (1926)	58
Clap Yo' Hands (1926)	62
Do-Do-Do (1926)	67
Someone To Watch Over Me (1926)	71
Preludes For Piano (1926)	76
Funny Face (1927)	77
'S Wonderful (1927)	81
He Loves And She Loves (1927)	85
My One And Only (1927)	89
The Babbitt And The Bromide (1927)	94
I've Got A Crush On You (1927)	99
An American In Paris (1928)	103
Liza (1929)	105
Soon (1930)	109
Strike Up The Band (1930)	113
Bidin' My Time (1930)	119
Embraceable You (1930)	123
I Got Rhythm (1930)	127

But Not For Me (1930)	131
Blah-Blah-Blah (1930)	135
Delishious (1930)	139
Wintergreen For President (1930)	144
Of Thee I Sing (1930)	149
Love Is Sweeping The Country (1930)	153
Who Cares? (1930)	157
Second Rhapsody (1932)	161
Cuban Overture (1932)	163
Lorelei (1933)	164
Isn't It A Pity? (1933)	169
My Cousin In Milwaukee (1933)	174
Mine (1933)	179
Let 'Em Eat Cake (1933)	185
Blue Blue Blue (1933)	191
Summertime (1935)	194
My Man's Gone Now (1935)	198
I Got Plenty O' Nuttin' (1935)	204
Bess, You Is My Woman Now (1935)	211
It Ain't Necessarily So (1935)	219
I Loves You Porgy (1935)	225
By Strauss (1936)	232
Let's Call The Whole Thing Off (1937)	237
They All Laughed (1937)	243
They Can't Take That Away From Me (1937)	249
A Foggy Day (1937)	254
Nice Work If You Can Get It (1937)	258
Love Is Here To Stay (1938)	263
Love Walked In (1938)	267
The Back Bay Polka (1946)	271
For You, For Me, For Evermore (1946)	275
Gershwin At The Keyboard	279

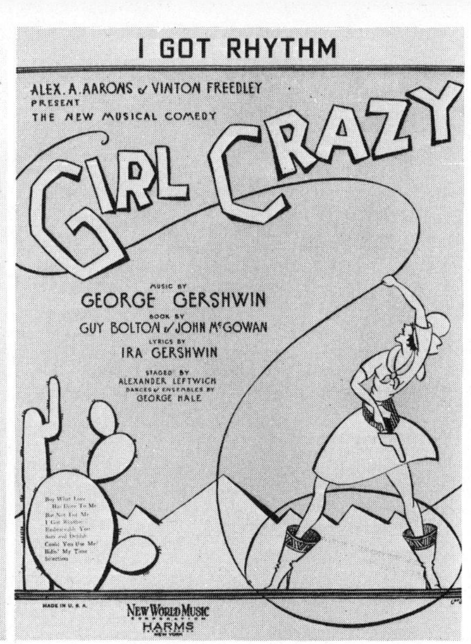

George singing excerpts from Porgy and Bess *(1934).*

During a cross-country tour, in Syracuse, N.Y. (1934).

A devoted golfer, George practices putting in Florida (1930).

INTRODUCTION

When Walt Whitman heard America singing, he heard the varied carols of individuals, "Each singing what belongs to him or her and to none else." For the last half-century we haven't had to be so self-reliant musically, for we have had, among others, George and Ira Gershwin to write the uncommon carols that we sing in common. They have provisioned us with a singular kind of American song that—all around the world—has epitomized the American scene.

From the beginning the Gershwin brothers thought of themselves as Americans. Although art may be international and unbounded, the impulse that sparked a Gershwin creation was markedly a part of our national tempo. In the twenties George and Ira saw the wistful irony that lay beneath apparent prosperity and jubilation; in the depression of the thirties they found hope and sunshine behind every cloud of grey. Maybe their essential Americanism is what Scott Fitzgerald labeled a first-class intelligence: the ability to hold opposing ideas in the mind at the same time and function. The words and music of the Gershwins enrich our civilization by helping us to see beyond appearances to that harder granite which supports the American dream.

George and Ira always thought of their work as grounded in, and growing out of, its time. Thus they began in 1918 proposing that "The Real American Folk Song Is a Rag," but they soon agreed that that was not the only answer—even though Nora Bayes delivered their finding with her legendary authority in *Ladies First.* For the next twenty years the Gershwins made the 32-bar song respond as it seldom had before. The standards that the brothers set for themselves produced songs that remain standards for us all.

In 1924—the year of their first collaborative Broadway show—George braved the concert hall as composer-soloist with *Rhapsody in Blue.* For the rest of his brief life he wrote both show scores and concert works with the diligence and delight that sum up his character. In *Strike Up the Band* (1927) George and Ira put politics to music; they perfected this amalgam with *Of Thee I Sing* (1931), the first musical to win a Pulitzer Prize. And then in 1935 came *Porgy and Bess,* which the Gershwins wrote with DuBose Heyward. Throughout the world it is considered *The* American Opera.

Porgy and Bess also emphasized the non exclusivity of the brothers' collaboration. ("Summertime" and "My Man's Gone Now," for example, were by George and DuBose.) From the beginning, the brothers often worked with others. "Swanee" is George's collaboration with Irving Caesar; "Somebody Loves Me," with B. G. DeSylva and Ballard Macdonald. During George's life, Ira set lyrics for, among other composers, Vernon Duke, Harold Arlen, Phil Charig and Harry Warren. And after George's death he continued to work with Arlen (*A Star Is Born*) and Warren (*The Barkleys of Broadway*); he also wrote with Kurt Weill *(Lady in the Dark),* Aaron Copland *(North Star)* and Jerome Kern *(Cover Girl).* And from George's unused tunes Ira constructed two posthumous scores for films—for the greatest pleasure he has had in his creative life came from collaborating with his brother. Indeed, when we think of the great Gershwin songs we think, with few exceptions, of this unique fraternal collaboration. The invaluable contribution of Ira is impressively, but simply, proven: most of those Gershwin songs which have withstood the changing tides of taste are anchored to his words. He brought to the art of lyric-writing a new literacy, craftsmanship, wit and perception that quickly won him the admiration of his peers and placed him in the pantheon of songwriters.

There have been Gershwin folios and songbooks before—we remember in particular a handsome one that George himself compiled in 1932, another that Ira annotated in 1960. But there has never been one like this: a chronological words-and-music "autobiography" covering all the years of the Gershwins' collaboration. This volume was the idea of Irving Brown who, as a music publisher, has long enjoyed friendship with Ira and a close association with the songs of the Gershwins. This folio's inclusion of excerpts from George's concert works as well as the *Piano Preludes* reminds us that George moved—and he did it gracefully—between the two worlds of "popular" and "serious" music, to the great enrichment of Musical America. (It might be noted that the two adjectives applied to music in the previous sentence meant nothing to him; George Gershwin made music and left the semantics of criticism to others.)

The exceptional form of this collection underscores the evolution of the Gershwins. The "hits" are included, of course; but so are those special gems that once could be seen only in the troves of a Gershwin specialist. Now that the works of the Gershwins rightfully are a part of our cultural heritage, all of the songs—hit or rarity—have taken on historical importance. This importance might appear to be a heavy burden for so fragile a construction as a 32-bar song, but each has stood up to the test of time and remains as sparkling in the hearing as it is haunting in the memory.

Happily among the collector's items now available herein are the early "Real American Folk Song" and the twenties party song, "Mischa, Yascha, Toscha, Sascha"—George and Ira's tribute to their friends, Messrs. Elman, Heifetz, Seidel and Jacobsen. "The Babbit and the Bromide" reminds us that as early as 1927 the Gershwins were making wry social commentary in their songs, a practice that flowered in the political operettas. Their views on the cliché-filled "ballad" of Tin Pan Alley are ingeniously defined in "Blah, Blah, Blah"—an attitude which, incidentally, made Ira Gershwin a particularly severe critic of his own ballads. (He was never satisfied with "Love Walked In" because "it doesn't say anything new." Earlier he had grumbled in a Yip Harburg-Harold Arlen collaboration, "What can you say in a love song that hasn't been said before?"). George too liked to spoof the accepted and overdone, thus "By Strauss," a spoof which—like all such Gershwin attacks—is so good-humored that we forget the intention and love the tribute.

A very special feature of *The New York Times Gershwin Years in Song* is "Gershwin at the Keyboard." In 1932 George prepared piano arrangements of eighteen of his songs, writing down the improvisations he liked to perform for his friends and his own amusement. These first appeared in *George Gershwin's Song Book,* now long out-of-print and a true collector's item. The transcriptions sum up the Gershwin style (in études, if you will) wherein those characteristics of his music-making—in melody, rhythm and harmony—are scored so that everyone can have "A Gershwin Evening," with the evoked presence of the composer himself at the keyboard.

"Gone, Gone, Gone" may be true of Charleston's world of *Porgy and Bess,* but it is scarcely a truth about George Gershwin himself. What, then, are the dates of the Gershwin years? Perhaps they commence with that day in the early 1890's when Morris Gershwin, George and Ira's father, first saw the Statue of Liberty and lost his heart to America, When do they conclude? They seem unending. How strange to think that 1973 would have been the seventy-fifth birthday of that brashly beguiling youth—but the fact is indisputable. It is so indisputable that the U.S. Postal Service was prompted to mark the occasion by issuing a handsome commemorative stamp in February 1973 that carries the Gershwin name and George's photo—and the evocation of its American sound around the world. But Gershwin has never been tied to a special moment or the temporal limits of occasion. While we can put this folio upon the piano and play and hear and feel, we are ever in The Gershwin Years, sensing not only the tempo of our civilization but that most abiding of our emotions: love. Like love itself, and like the land they sang of and loved, the Gershwins and their songs are indeed here to stay.

April, 1973

Edward Jablonski
New York, New York

Lawrence D. Stewart
Beverly Hills, Calif.

THE REAL AMERICAN FOLK SONG (Is A Rag)

Lyrics by IRA GERSHWIN

Music by GEORGE GERSHWIN

Em B7 Em G7 C G7+5
think of I - tal - ian skies. Each na - tion has a cre -
may be dis - tinc - tive, yet They lack a some-thing: a
C G7+5 C E7(♭5) A7 D9 G7 C C(B bass)
a - tive vein O - rig - i - nat - ing a na - tive strain, With folk songs plain-tive and
cer - tain snap, The tem - po tick-lish that makes you tap, The in - vi - ta - tion to
Am7 D9 C G7 C G7
oth - ers gay In their own pe - cu - liar way. A - mer - i - can folk songs, I
ag - i - tate And leave the rest to fate. A rag - gy re - frain an - y -
A♭(G♭ bass) A7 Dm7 G7
feel, Have a much strong - er ap - peal.
time Sends me a mes - sage sub - lime.

Tempo di Fox Trot
Refrain:
C G7 C7 Fm6
The Real A-mer-i-can Folk Song is a rag,
mf
C D9 G7
A men-tal jag, A rhyth-mic
F7 C B G7 C
ton-ic for the chron-ic blues. The crit-ics called it a
Eb7 Ab Eb7
joke song, but now They've

A♭
D7
G Am6 G Am6
changed their tune — and they like it some - how.
G
F
Cmaj7 Cdim
Dm7
A7
— For it's in - oc - u - lat - ed with a syn - co - pat - ed sort of
D7
D9
G
Dm7
me - ter, Sweet - er Than a class - ic strain.
C
A7
D7
G7
G7+5
Boy! You can't — re-main Still and qui - et, For it's a ri - ot! The

C G7 C7 F D9 Cdim
Real A - mer - i - can Folk Song is like a Foun - tain of Youth: - You
C Cdim G7 Gdim Cm6 E7 E7(♭5) A7(sus) A7
taste, and it e - lates_you, And then in - vig - or - ates_ you. The
F6 C B F6 Dm G7+5
Real A - mer - i - can Folk Song,___ A mas- ter stroke song, is a
1.
C G7 Dm7 G7
rag. The
2.
C G7 C
rag.
3
f

George at the time of his first musical, Half Past Eight (1918).

Self Portrait in an Opera Hat *by George (1932).*

My Body *by Ira (1932).*

SWANEE

Lyrics by IRVING CAESAR

Music by GEORGE GERSHWIN

B♭
Fm
B♭
Fm
C7
Some - how I feel Your love was real,
Fm
C
C7
D♭dim
C7
Near you I long to be,
sfz
Fm
B♭m
Fm
Gm7
C7
The birds are sing - ing, It is song - time,
mf
Fm
G7
B♭m7
Fm
The ban - jos strum-min' soft and low,
mf

B♭ Fm B♭ Fm C7
I know that you Yearn for me too;
Fm C7 Fm Fm7 G7 D♭m6
Swan - ee You're call - ing me.
sfz
Refrain:
F F+5
Swan - ee How I love you, How I love you
mp - mf
B♭ Gm7 C9 F Gm7 F C F C7
My dear old Swan - ee; I'd give the

F Db7 C9 Gm D7 Db7
world to be A - mong the
C9 F C9 Am E C7
folks in D - I - X - I - E - ven know my
F F+5
Mam - my's Wait - ing for me, Pray - ing for me
Bb Gm7 C9 F Gm7 F C F C7
Down by the Swan - ee, The folks up

F
F+5
B♭
F+5
Gm
F♯dim
north
will
see me no more
When
C7
Dm
C
B♭
Am
C7
F
1.
Bdim
C7
Cdim
C7
C9+5
I go to the Swan - ee shore.
2. To Trio
Spoken:
(I'll be hap - py
I'll be hap - py)
3.
D♭7
B♭7
F
TRIO
C7
F
Swan - ee,
Swan - ee,
mp - mf

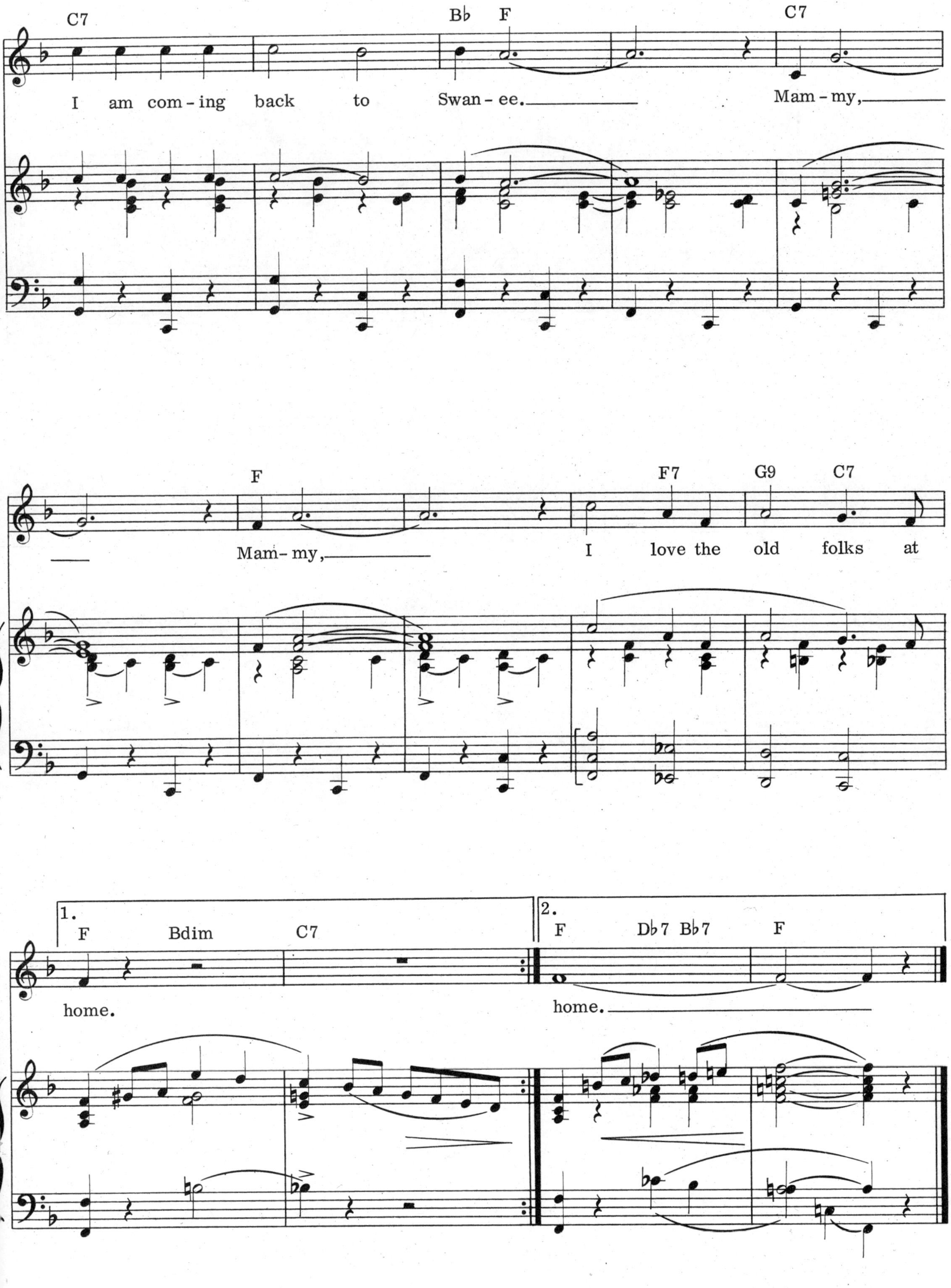

C7 B♭ F C7

I am com-ing back to Swan-ee. Mam-my,

F F7 G9 C7

Mam-my, I love the old folks at

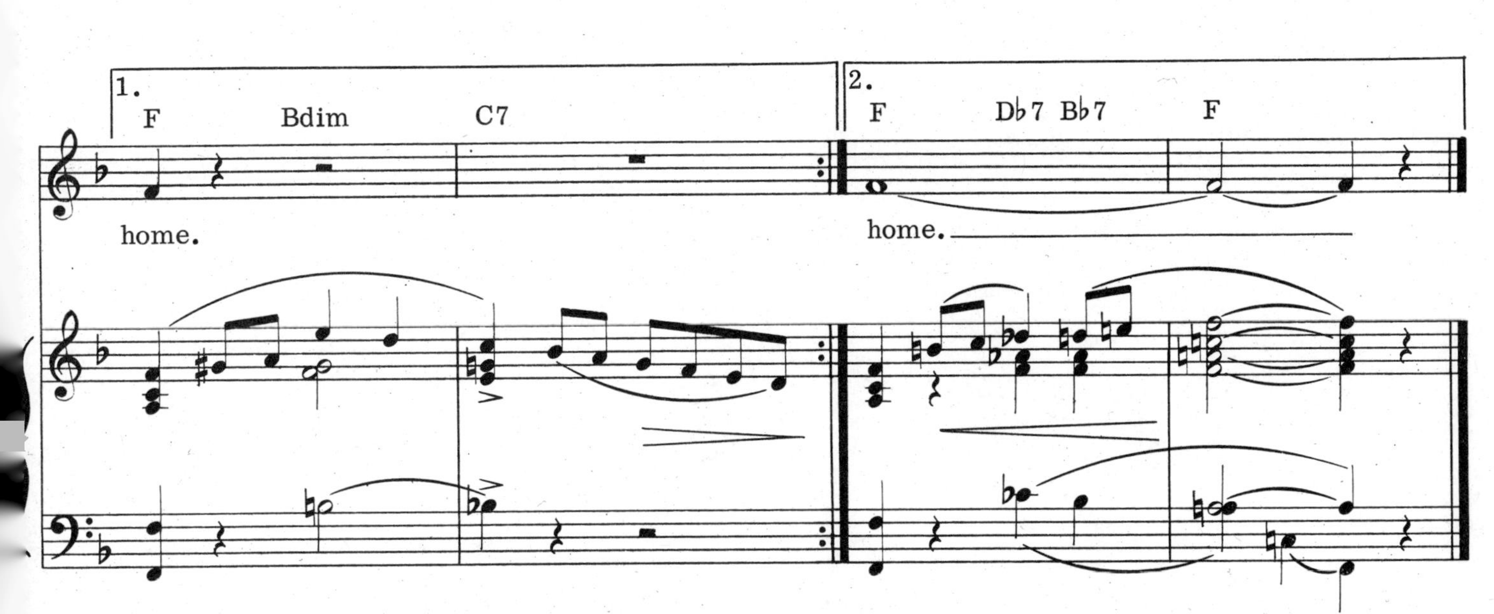

MISCHA, YASCHA, TOSCHA, SASCHA

Lyrics by ARTHUR FRANCIS (Ira Gershwin) | Music by GEORGE GERSHWIN

When we were three years old or so, We all be-gan to play the
fid-dle In dark-est Rus-sia. When we be-gan our notes were sour
Un-til a man, Pro-fes-sor Auer, Set out to show us, one and
all, How we could pack them in, in Car-ne-gie Hall.

Refrain:

Temp-r'a- men - tal O - ri - en - tal Gen-tle-men are we,
p
f
dim.

Mis - cha Yas - cha, Tos - cha Sas - cha, Fid-dle le fid-dle le dee.

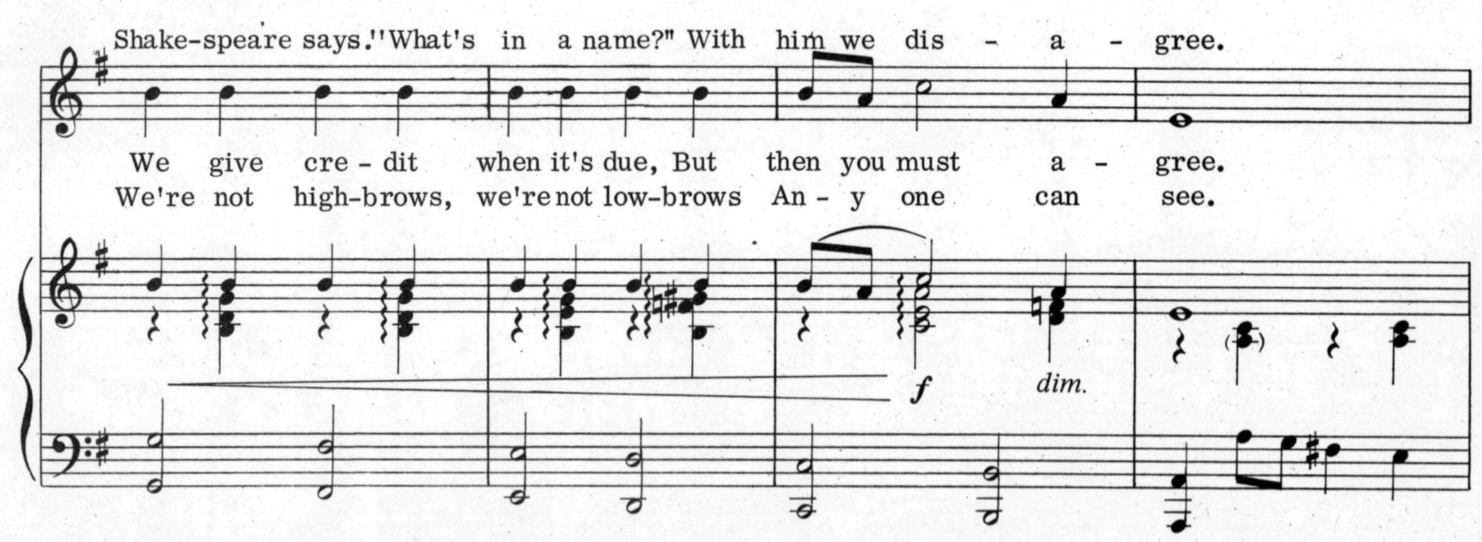
Shake-speare says."What's in a name?" With him we dis - a - gree.
We give cre - dit when it's due, But then you must a - gree.
We're not high-brows, we're not low-brows An - y one can see.
f
dim.

Names like Sam - my, Max or Moe Nev - er bring the
That out - side of dear old Fritz All the fid - dle
You don't have to use a chart To see we're He - brows
heav - y dough, Just
con - cert hits are
from the start, Just
Mis - cha Yas - cha, Tos - cha Sas - cha,
1.
2.
Fid-dle le fid-dle le dee.
dee.
3
3

I'LL BUILD A STAIRWAY TO PARADISE

Lyrics by B. G. DeSYLVA
ARTHUR FRANCIS (Ira Gershwin)

Music by GEORGE GERSHWIN

F7
Bb
A7
Ab7
G7
F#7
F7
Of the dance that car-ry you through
The gates of Heav-en.
Bb
F#7
B
It's mad-ness
To be al-ways sit-ting a-round in sad-ness,
sf
G7
C
Ab7
When you could be learn-ing the steps of glad-ness.
You'll be hap-py when you can
Db
C7
B7
Bb7
A7
Ab7
G7
G9-5
do
just
six
or
sev-en.
Be-gin
to-day!
You'll

Dm7 G9 C G9+5 C6 G9+5
find it nice, The quick-est way to Par - a-dise.
E F#m7 B7 Em Em7 C#dim G7
When you prac-tice, Here's the thing to know, Simp-ly say as you go:
Con spirito
Refrain:
C G7 C7 G7 C
I'll Build A Stair-way To Par-a-dise, With a new step ev-'ry
p-f
C7 F C7 F7 F6
day! I'm going to get there at an-y price; Stand a-

C Cdim G7sus4 G7 G9+5 C
side, I'm on my way! I've got the blues, And up a-
Ab7
bove it's so fair. Shoes, Go on and car-ry me there!
C G7+5 C7 C♯dim
I'll Build A Stair - way To Par - a - dise, With a
D7 Dm7 G7
1. C F♯dim G9
2. C Ab9 C
new step ev-'ry day. day.

SOMEBODY LOVES ME

Lyrics by BALLARD MACDONALD & B. G. DeSYLVA · Music by GEORGE GERSHWIN

G
Am
D7
G6
G
Am
D7
G6
To my great re - gret
Some - one has up - set
Am7
D7sus4
D7
G7
Em
Cm6
D7
Em
Em6
Heav - en's pret - ty pro - gram for we've nev - er met; I'm
Bm
Bm6
E7
Em7
A7
D7
D7+5
clutch - ing at straws, just be - cause I may meet her yet.
poco rit.

Refrain:
G Am7 Am D7 G C7
Some - bod - y Loves Me, I won - der who,
p-f a tempo
G C9 Am7 D7 G D7-9
I won-der who she can be;
G Am7 Am D7 G A7
Some - bod - y Loves Me I wish I knew,
Bm C#7-9 C#m7 F#7 Bm E7
Who can she be wor-ries me,
For ev - 'ry

Am
Dm6
Am
Dm6
Am
girl who pass - es me I shout, Hey! may - be,
Em7
A7
Em7
A7
D7
D+5
You were meant to be my lov - ing ba - by;
G
Am7
Am D7
G
C7
G
Em7
Some - bod - y Loves Me, I won-der who, May -
Am7
D7
1.
G
D7
2.
G
Am D9
G
be it's you.
you.
mf
rit. e dim.
fz

FASCINATING RHYTHM

Lyrics by IRA GERSHWIN

Music by GEORGE GERSHWIN

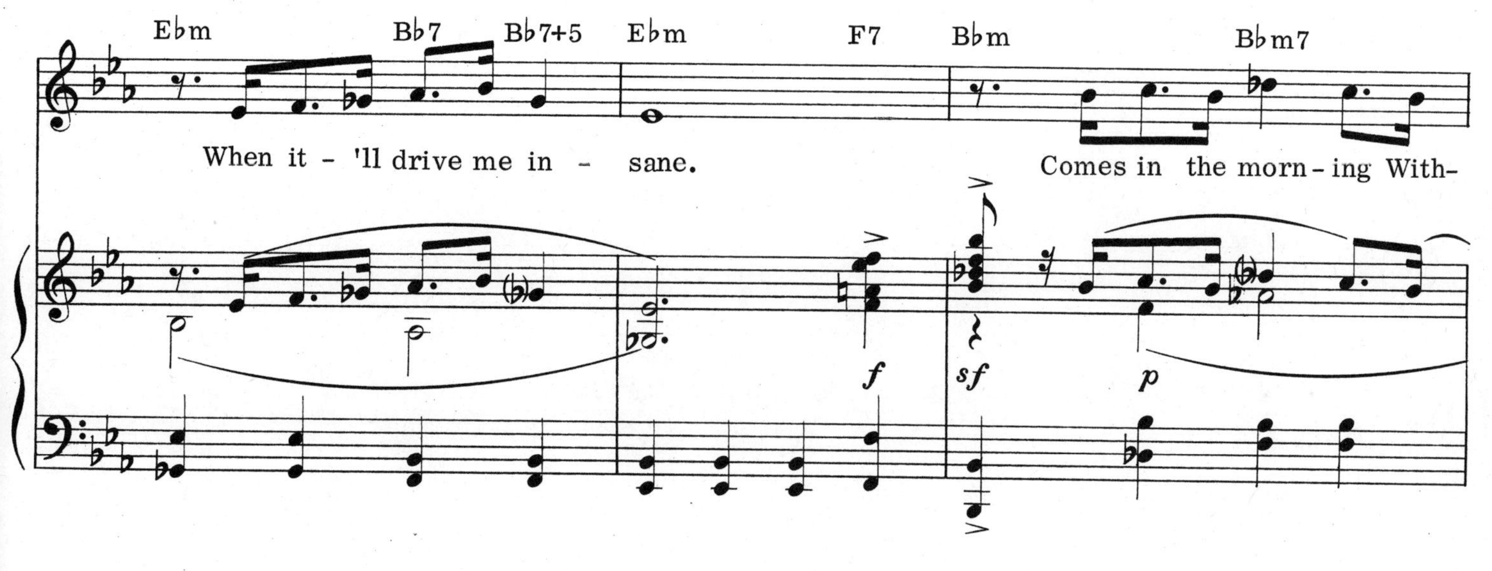
Ebm
Bb7
Bb7+5
Ebm
F7
Bbm
Bbm7
When it - 'll drive me in - sane.
Comes in the morn - ing With-
f
sf
p
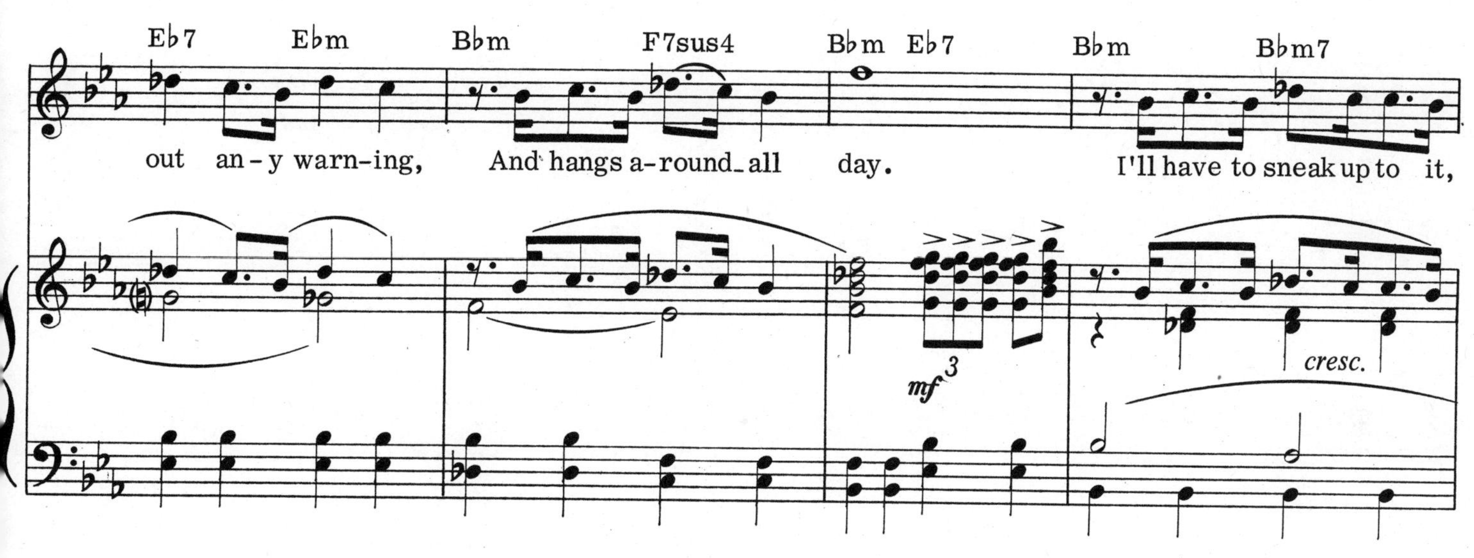
Eb7
Ebm
Bbm
F7sus4
Bbm
Eb7
Bbm
Bbm7
out an - y warn - ing,
And hangs a - round_all
day.
I'll have to sneak up to it,
mf
cresc.

Eb
Ebm
F7
Bb
Some - day, and speak up to it,
I hope it lis - tens when I
say:

Refrain:
Bb7 Ab Bb7 Ab Bb7 Ab Bb7 Ab
Fas - ci - nat - ing Rhy - thm You've got me on the go! Fas - ci -
p
Bb7 Ab Bb7 Ab Bb7 Eb7 Db Eb7 Db
nat-ing Rhy-thm I'm all a - qui - ver. What a mess you're mak-ing! The
Eb7 Db Eb7 Db Eb7 Db Eb7 Db Eb7
neigh-bors want to know why I'm al-ways shak-ing Just like a fliv - ver.
Ab Fm7 Gm Bb9+5 Eb
Each morn - ing I get up with the sun,

Eb7
Cm
Cm7 Cm7-5
F
F7-9
(Start a - hop- ping, nev - er stop-ping)
To find at night, no work_ has been
Bb7
C#dim
Bb7
Ab
Bb7
Ab
done.
I know that once it did - n't mat - ter But
Bb7
Ab
Bb7
Ab
Bb7
Ab
Bb7
Ab
Bb7
now you're do-ing wrong; When you start to pat- ter, I'm so un - hap - py.
Eb7
Db
Eb7
Db
Eb7
Db
Eb7
Db
Won't you take a day off? De - cide to run a - long Some-where

Eb7 Db Eb7 Db Eb7 Ab
far a-way off, And make it snap - py! Oh, how I
mf
Dm7-5 G7 Cm Bb Ebmaj7 F7
long to be the man I used to be!
Bb7 Ab Bb7 Ab Bb7 F7 Bb7
1. Eb
Fas-ci-nat-ing Rhy-thm, Oh, won't you stop pick - ing on me!
p
E D C B
2. Eb Ab Cm Eb Fm Ab Eb
me!
mf
cresc.
sf

George with musical comedy actress Olive Brady (1928).

George and Ira arriving in Hollywood to compose film songs for Rogers and Astaire (1936).

George in Miami (1930).

Ira on the Goldwyn lot where The Goldwyn Follies, *George's last film, was shot (1937).*

OH, LADY BE GOOD

Lyrics by IRA GERSHWIN

Music by GEORGE GERSHWIN

D7(G bass)
G
D7(G bass)
G
F♯m7
B7
I must win some win-some miss; Can't go on like this.
Win-ter's gone, and now it's Spring! Love! where is thy sting?
pp
E
F♯m7
B7
E
Amaj7
E
F♯7
B7
E
D7
I could blos-som out I know, With some-bod-y just like you, so,
If some-bod-y won't re-spond, I'm go-ing to end it all, so,
p
mf
rit.
Slow (gracefully)
Refrain:
G
D7
G
C9
G
G♯dim
D7
Oh, sweet and love-ly la-dy, be good! Oh, La-dy Be Good
Oh, sweet and love-ly la-dy, be good! Oh, La-dy Be Good
p-mf
G
D7
G
C9
to me! I am so awf'-ly
to me! I am so awf'-ly

G G♯dim D7 G G7
mis-un-der- stood, So la - dy be good to me.
mis-un-der- stood, So la - dy be good to me.
C D9 C G D7 Em B+5 Em A9
Oh, please have some pit - y, I'm all a - lone in this big
This is tu - lip weath - er, So let's put two and two to-
mf molto espress.
Am7 D7 Bm Am7 A7-5 G D7 G C9 G G♯dim
cit - y. I tell you I'm just a lone - some babe in the wood, So
geth - er. I tell you I'm just a lone - some babe in the wood, So
p
D7 1. G D7 Am7 D7 2. G C9 G
La - dy, Be Good to me!
La - dy, Be Good to me!

THE MAN I LOVE

Lyrics by IRA GERSHWIN
French Lyrics by EMILIA RENAUD
Music by GEORGE GERSHWIN

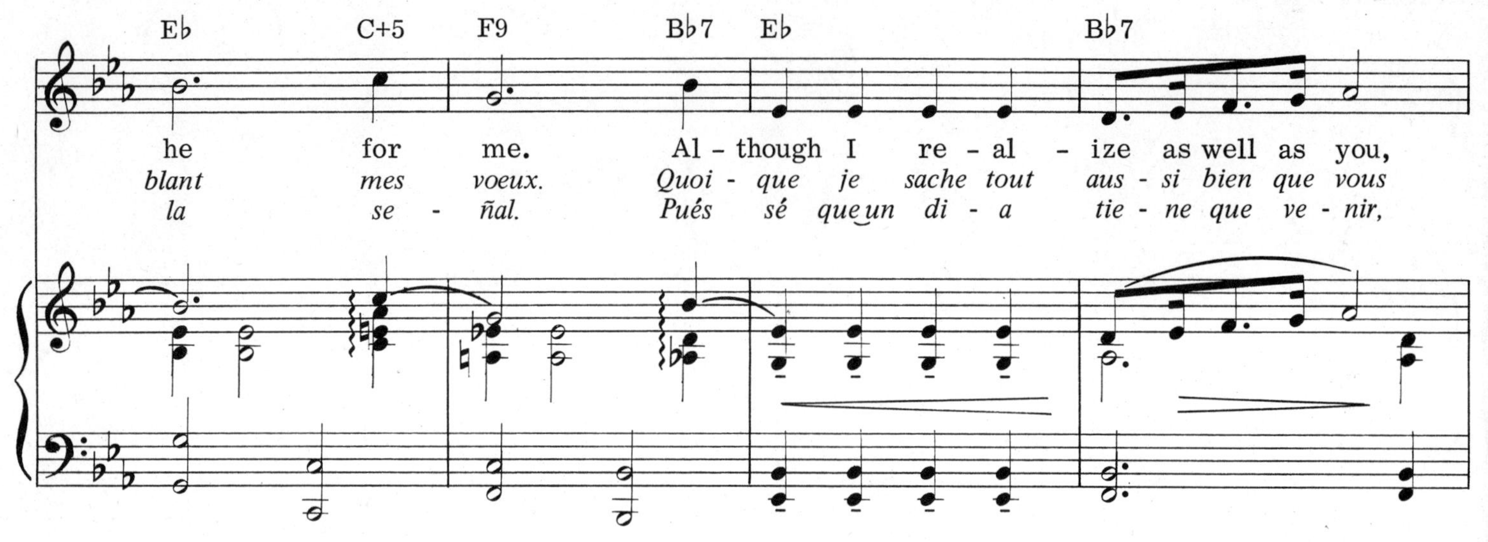
Eb C+5 F9 Bb7 Eb Bb7
he for me. Al - though I re - al - ize as well as you,
blant mes voeux. Quoi - que je sache tout aus - si bien que vous
la se - ñal. Pués sé que un di - a tie - ne que ve - nir,

Gm Cm Cdim Bb
It is sel - dom that a dream comes true, To me it's
Qu'un beau rê - ve n'est qu'un dé - sir fou C'est j'en suis
E - se gran a - mor que yo so - ñé; ¡Mi sue - ño a -

F7-9 Bb Bbdim Ab Bb7
clear That he'll ap - pear.
sûre De bon au - gure.
zul! ¡Mi gran que - rer!
dim.
poco rall.

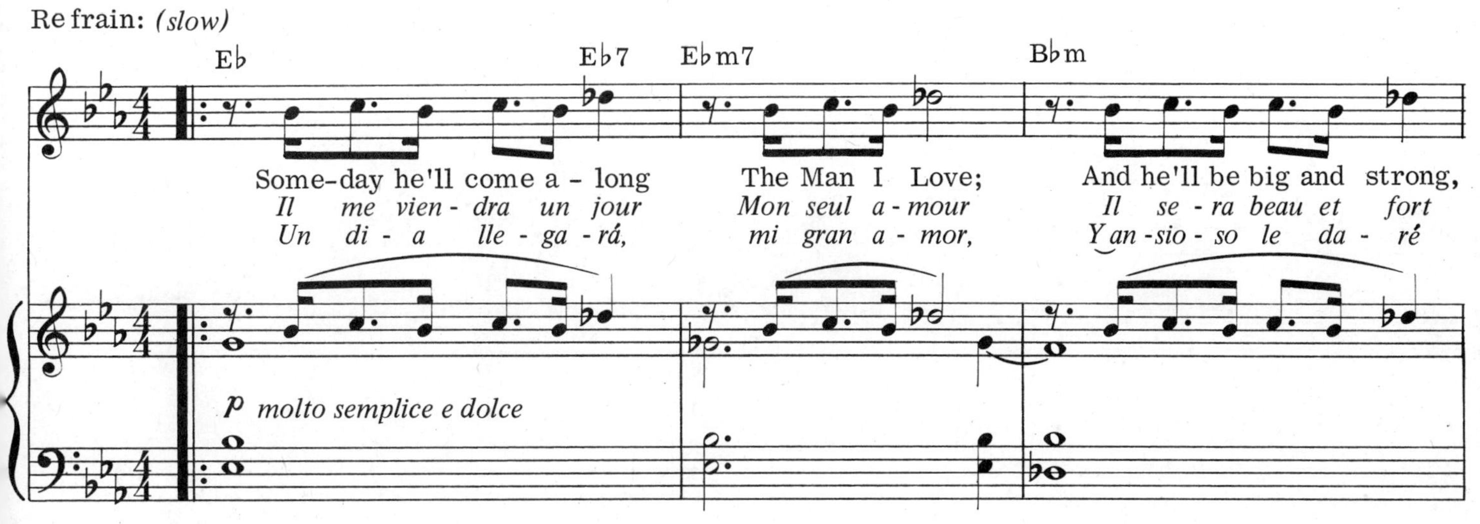
Re frain: (slow)
Eb
Eb7
Ebm7
Bbm
Some-day he'll come a - long
The Man I Love;
And he'll be big and strong,
Il me vien - dra un jour
Mon seul a - mour
Il se - ra beau et fort
Un di - a lle - ga - rá,
mi gran a - mor,
Y an - sio - so le da - ré
p molto semplice e dolce

C7+5
C7
Fm7-5
Bb7
The Man I Love;
And when he comes my way,
I'll do my best to
Un vrai gail - lard,
Et quand sur mon che - min,
Il vou - dra me ten -
Mi tier - no a - mor...
Y lo - co de an - sie - dad,
Mi ser, al fin, le en -

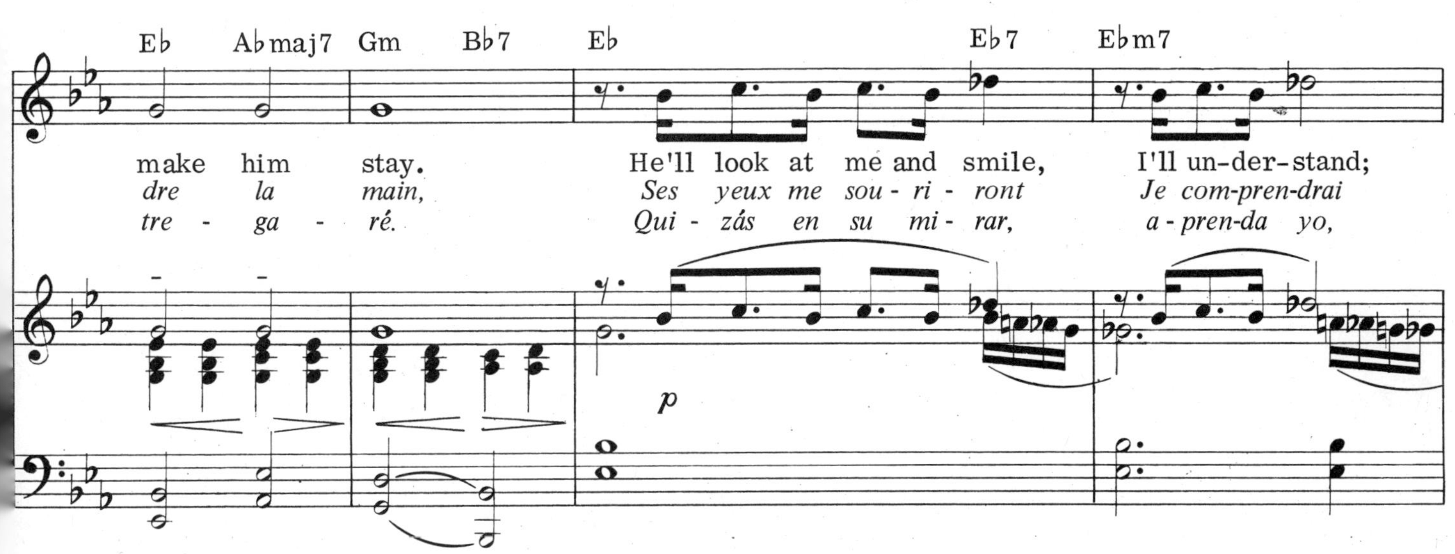
Eb
Abmaj7
Gm
Bb7
Eb
Eb7
Ebm7
make him stay.
He'll look at me and smile,
I'll un - der - stand;
dre la main,
Ses yeux me sou - ri - ront
Je com - pren - drai
tre - ga - ré.
Qui - zás en su mi - rar,
a - pren - da yo,
p

B♭m
C7+5
C7
And in a lit - tle while
Et sans hé - si - ta - tion
Por - qué fué que es - pe - ré
He'll take my hand;
Je ré - pon - drai.
por es - te a - mor;
Fm7-5
B♭7
Fm7 B♭7
E♭
A♭
And though it seems ab - surd,
Bien que ce soit fo - lie,
Vi - vien - do sin a - mor,
I know we both won't say a
En - tre nous pas un mot n'est
So - ñan - do siem - pre por los
E♭ Adim A♭7 G7
Cm
Cm7
D7
Ddim
word.
dit
dos.
May - be I shall meet him Sun - day, May - be
Le ver - rais - je lun - di, mar - di? Ou peut
Pue - de ser que lle - gue un lu - nes, Pue - de
mp
poco
espr.
Cm
G7
Cm
Cm7
Mon - day may - be not;
être en - core jeu - di?
ser que no se - rá...
Still I'm sure to meet him
J'ai la cer - ti - tu - de
Pe - ro es - toy se - gu - ro el

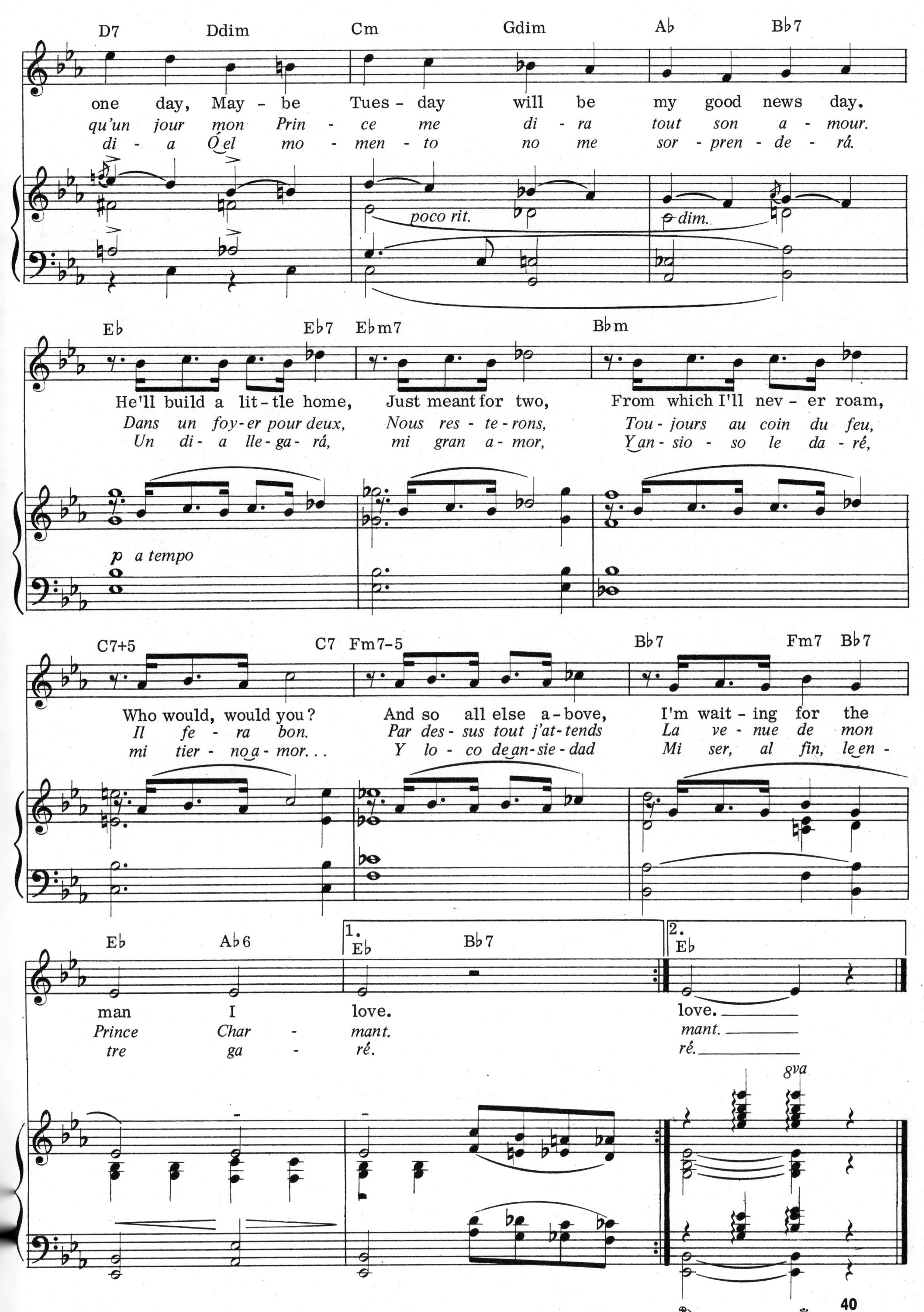

D7 Ddim Cm Gdim A♭ B♭7
one day, May - be Tues - day will be my good news day.
qu'un jour mon Prin - ce me di - ra tout son a - mour.
di - a O el mo - men - to no me sor - pren - de - rá.
poco rit.
dim.
E♭ E♭7 E♭m7 B♭m
He'll build a lit - tle home, Just meant for two, From which I'll nev - er roam,
Dans un foy - er pour deux, Nous res - te - rons, Tou - jours au coin du feu,
Un di - a lle - ga - rá, mi gran a - mor, Y an - sio - so le da - ré,
p a tempo
C7+5 C7 Fm7-5 B♭7 Fm7 B♭7
Who would, would you? And so all else a - bove, I'm wait - ing for the
Il fe - ra bon. Par des - sus tout j'at - tends La ve - nue de mon
mi tier - no a - mor... Y lo - co de an - sie - dad Mi ser, al fin, le en -
E♭ A♭6 1. E♭ B♭7 2. E♭
man I love. love.
Prince Char - mant. mant.
tre ga - ré. ré.
8va
Ped. *
40

RHAPSODY IN BLUE

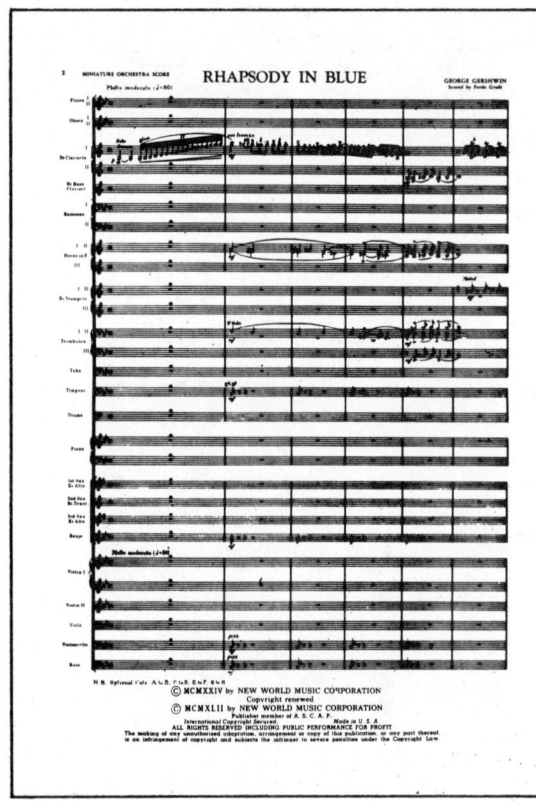

While it is customary, and indeed proper, to date the concert hall and "serious" Gershwin from the premiere of *Rhapsody in Blue* on February 12, 1924, he was in fact no stranger to the recital stage nor to concert music. Late in 1923, for example, he served as accompanist to the celebrated mezzo-soprano Eva Gauthier for the American portion of her "Recital of Ancient and Modern Music for Voice"—and stole the show with his pianistics. As early as 1920 his study for string quartet, *Lullaby,* was a favorite among his string playing friends (whose names may very well have been Mischa, Yascha, Toscha and Sascha). In the summer of 1922 he even attempted a one-act opera, *Blue Monday,* an interesting but not completely formed work—although an intimation of what would come in *Porgy and Bess.*

Paul Whiteman, the burgeoning "King of Jazz" (so crowned by press agentry and not by regal blood line), had conducted the single performance of *Blue Monday,* had been impressed by its composer and proceeded to put him on the spot (press agentry again) which led to the creation of *Rhapsody in Blue.* Hoping to exploit the twenties jazz rage, Whiteman had planned to present a concert which he called "An Experiment in Modern Music" at staid Aeolian Hall in New York City, home of the classics. While this was in the talking stage he and Gershwin had discussed the possibility of an extended Gershwin work for the concert. Then it was forgotten. Soon another band leader announced that he was planning a concert of jazz in which he hoped to prove something or other. This galvanized Whiteman who quickly proclaimed his concert would take place instantly. The first word Gershwin received of this change in plan was when his brother Ira read him a newspaper item about Whiteman's "Experiment" in which it was noted that George Gershwin was writing a "jazz concerto" for the event. This was news, indeed, to Gershwin.

At that moment—it was February 3, 1924 and the concert was scheduled for February 12—Gershwin was deep in the pre-Broadway birthing pains of a musical; he could hardly see his way clear to work up a "concerto" in the month or so ahead. Somehow when he phoned Whiteman, the band leader managed to persuade him he could in fact produce something in time for the concert. They compromised on the less exacting form of a rhapsody for which Gershwin would provide a piano version, from which Ferdé Grofe, Whiteman's arranger-orchestrator, would work up an orchestral score.

Three days later Gershwin was at work on what he had initially called "American Rhapsody"—the final title was suggested by Ira Gershwin after an afternoon of visiting art galleries. He worked between rehearsals, trips to Boston to see how the new show was evolving and other travails. The work was complete—more or less—in time for the concert, although several blank pages in the piano part were improvised by Gershwin during the performance.

The brash new work and its youthful composer were the sensations of the evening, both heralded and damned in the press (Gershwin and the critics rarely saw eye to eye). The impact of that single work (who remembers that Victor Herbert contributed a *Suite of Serenades?*) served to put American music on the culture map and the American composer among the celebrities of the Jazz Age: Carl Van Vechten, Charles Lindbergh, Scott Fitzgerald, Babe Ruth and, of course, Al Capone.

This extra-musical benefit accomplished much for our American music for it proved that "serious" music laced with popular themes and dance-band tricks and effects could be entertaining and intellectually satisfying, that American music did have a characteristic native "sound," that it could stand on its own in a concert hall and that its creator need not be a sour-visaged, forbidding self-styled Master but rather an attractive youngster who was approachable, likeable and gifted. With the birth of *Rhapsody in Blue* George Gershwin became a kind of symbol of American youth—an artist, at that—in an exciting, strident, awakening America of the twenties. Like the various culture heroes of the time, he captivated the American imagination—highbrow and low—for he had youth, fame, success (and a wonderful capacity for the enjoyment of it) and—following the furor in the wake of *Rhapsody in Blue*—an air of controversy about him.

George at his favorite spot: at the keyboard.

A Twenties Trio: Leonore Strunsky (later Mrs. Ira Gershwin), Ira Gershwin and Emily Paley (sister of Leonore).

An early, pre-twenties studio portrait of a budding composer.

LOOKING FOR A BOY

Lyrics by IRA GERSHWIN

Music by GEORGE GERSHWIN

G7 C Cdim G Em C♯m F♯7+5
five foot six or sev - en, And won't be hap - py till I'm on his
Bm Bm7-5 E7 Dm E7 Dm E Dm6
knee. I'll be blue un - til he comes my way,
mp
Em E7 A7 Ddim A7 E♭7 D7 Cm6 Dm D+5
Hope he takes the cue when I am say - ing:
Refrain:
G G6 G G6 Gm C9
I am just a lit - tle girl who's look - ing for a
p-f a tempo

G G6 Gm C9 D7 D9 G6
lit - tle boy Who's look - ing for a girl to love.
D9 G G6 G G6 Gm C9
Tell me please, where can he be, the lov - ing he who'll
G G6 Bm Bm6 F#7 F#9
bring to me The har - mo - ny I'm dream - ing
Bm E7+5 Am F6 E7
of. It - 'll be good - bye, I know,

Am Bm7-5 E7 Am Am6 Em
To my tale of woe, When he says "Hel -
D D9 D7-9 G G6 G G6
lo!" So I am just a lit - tle girl who's
p
Gm C9 G G6 Gm C9 D7 D9
look - ing for a lit - tle boy Who's look - ing for a girl to
1. G C9 D7 2. G
love! love!
sf

THAT CERTAIN FEELING

Lyrics by IRA GERSHWIN

Music by GEORGE GERSHWIN

Ab9 Ab7 Ab9 Bb Gm Cm7 F7 Bb Eb6 Bb7 Bbdim
Steve:
that's the way you feel, But tell me is it real - ly real? You gave me
Since you've come my way; Be - lieve it when you hear me say: You gave me

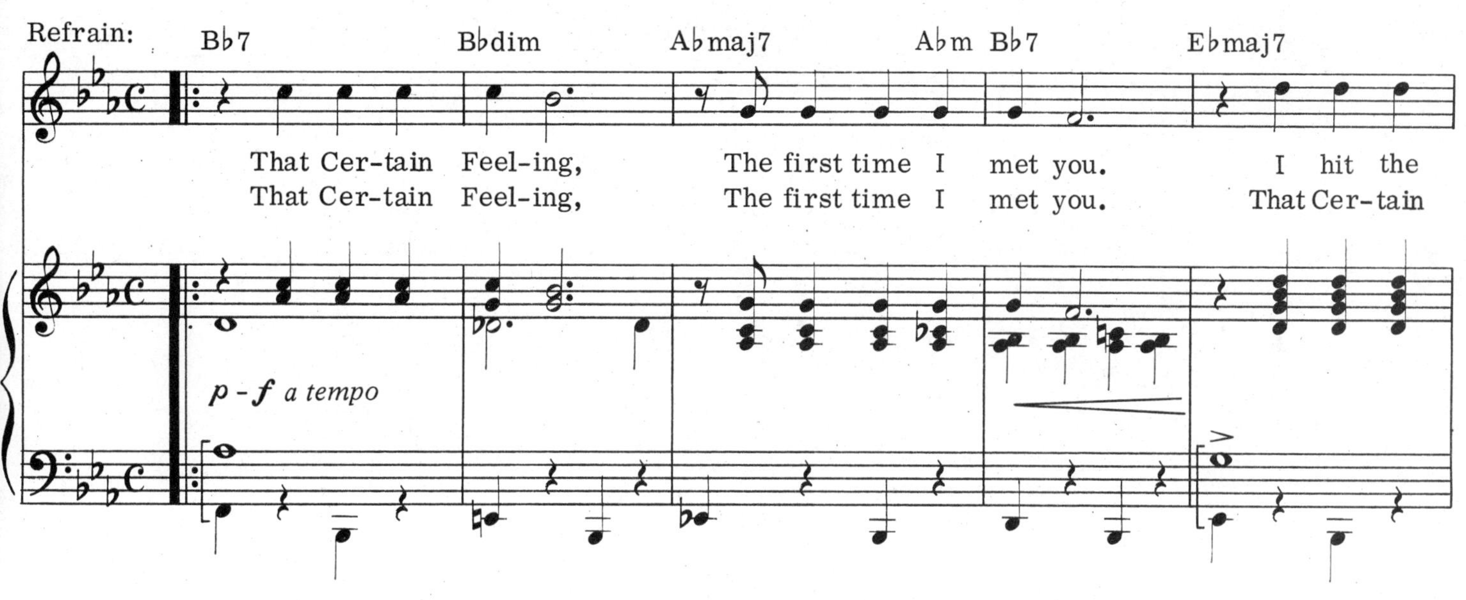

Refrain:
Bb7 Bbdim Abmaj7 Abm Bb7 Ebmaj7
That Cer-tain Feel-ing, The first time I met you. I hit the
That Cer-tain Feel-ing, The first time I met you. That Cer-tain
p - f a tempo

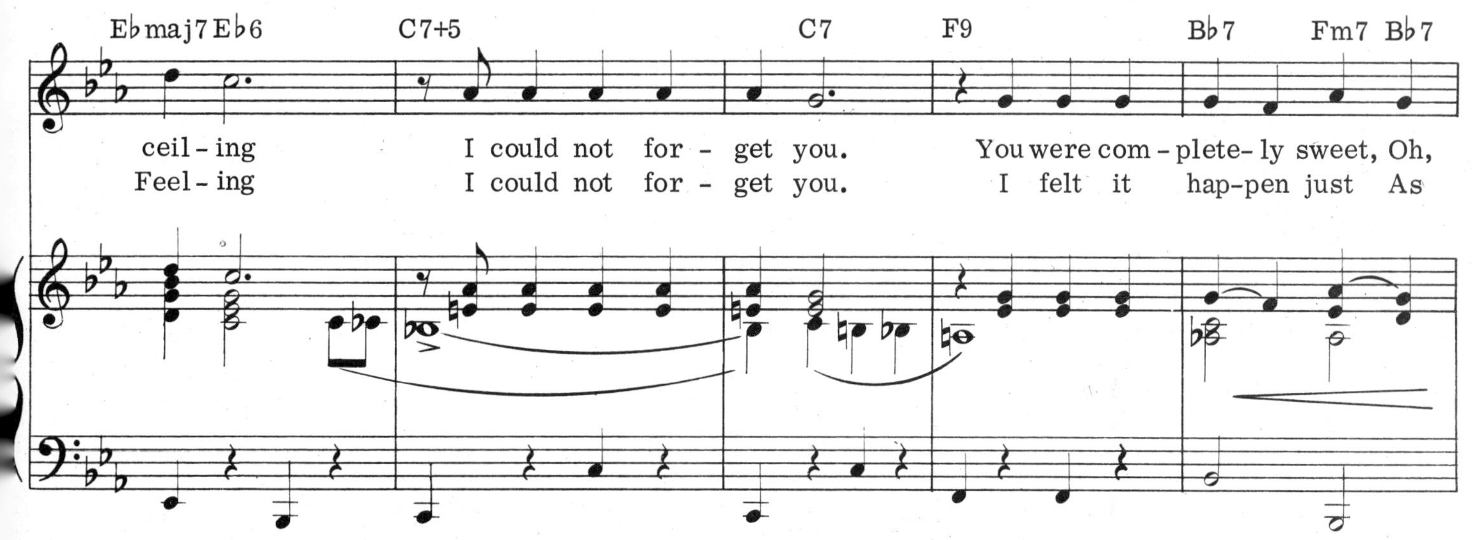

Ebmaj7 Eb6 C7+5 C7 F9 Bb7 Fm7 Bb7
ceil - ing I could not for - get you. You were com - plete- ly sweet, Oh,
Feel - ing I could not for - get you. I felt it hap-pen just As

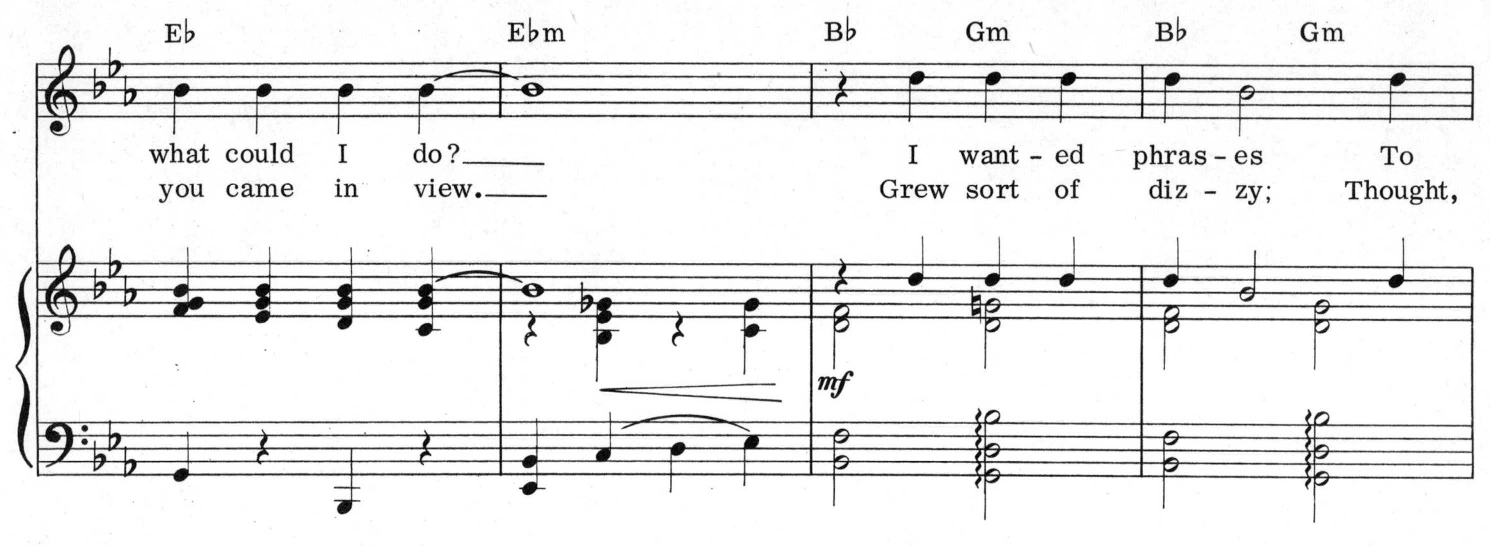
Eb Ebm Bb Gm Bb Gm
what could I do?
you came in view.
I want - ed phras - es To
Grew sort of diz - zy; Thought,
mf

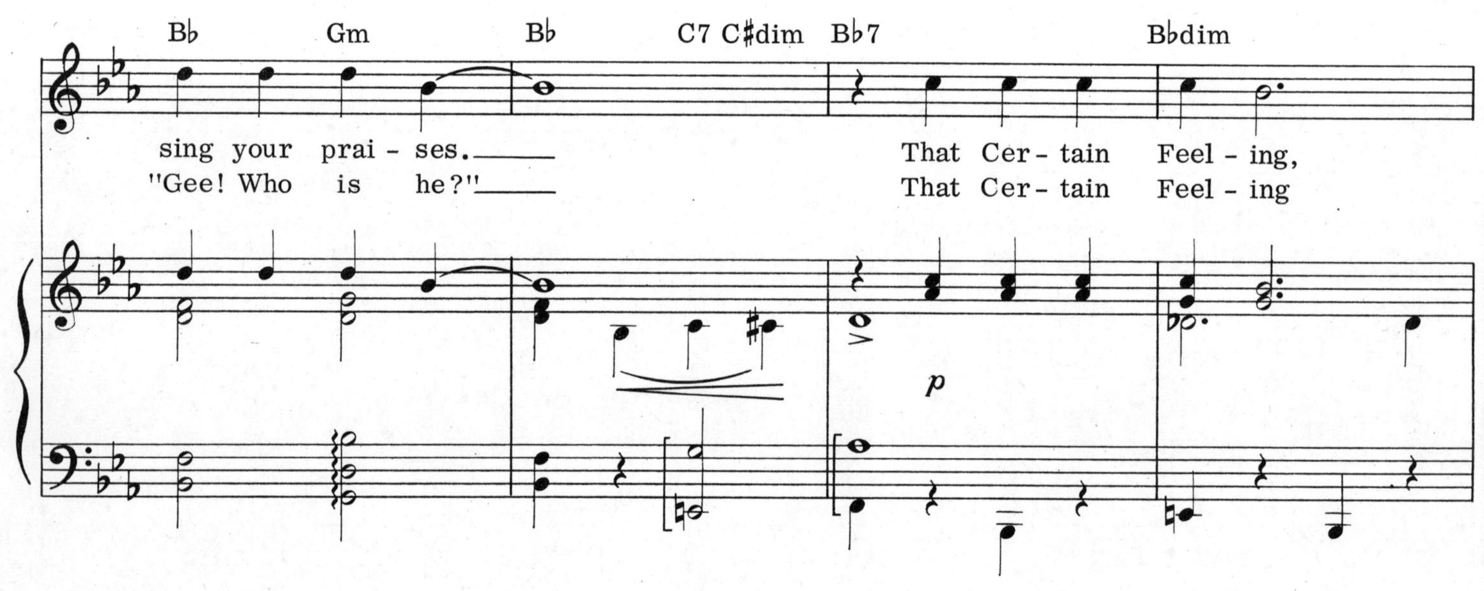
Bb Gm Bb C7 C#dim Bb7 Bbdim
sing your prai - ses.
"Gee! Who is he?"
That Cer - tain Feel - ing,
That Cer - tain Feel - ing
p

Abmaj7 Abm Bb7 Ebmaj7 Eb6
The one that they all love,
I'm here to con - fess, it
No use con - ceal - ing
Is so ap - peal - ing

A♭m6
G6 G7 Fm6 G7
C7
I've got what they call love.
Now we're to - geth - er Let's
No words can ex - press it.
I can - not hide it, I
cresc.
mf

F9
B♭7 B♭dim D♭m6
F9
B♭6 B♭7+5
find out wheth - er
You're feel - ing that feel - ing,
must con - fide it
I'm feel - ing that feel - ing,
p
pochett. rit.

1.
E♭ Cm E♭ E♭6 B♭7 B♭dim
2.
E♭ Cm E♭
too.
You gave me
too.
mf a tempo
poco rit.
mf
sf

SWEET AND LOW-DOWN

Lyrics by IRA GERSHWIN
Music by GEORGE GERSHWIN

Gm
Cm
F7
B♭7
E♭6
"blue."
They play noth-ing class-ic, oh no! down there;
mf
Am7-5
D7
Gm7
D9
D7
Gm
They crave noth-ing else but the low down there.
If you need a ton-ic,
dim.
p
A♭(G bass)
A(G bass)
D7
Cmaj7
F7-5
D7
And the need is chron-ic;
If you're in a cri-sis,
My ad-vice is:
molto cresc.
rit.
Refrain:
G
Grab a cab and go down To where the band is play-ing; Where
p-f a tempo
cresc.

G6
G♯dim
milk and hon - ey flow down, Where ev - 'ry - one is say - ing,
D
E♭
E
Dm7
D7+5
D7
G6
"Blow that Sweet And Low - Down!"
mf
E♭9
E♭7
G
(tu - tu!)
Bus - y as a bea - ver, You'll
p
G6
dance un - til you tot - ter; You're sure to get the fe - ver For

G♯dim
D E♭ E Dm7 D7+5 D7
noth-ing could be hot - ter, Oh, that Sweet And
mf
G6
B7
Low - Down!
Phi - los-o-pher or dea-con, You
mp
Bm7(E bass) E7(B bass) Bm7(E bass) E7(B bass)
sim-ply have to weak-en. Hear those shuff-ling feet!
Em7add11 A9 Em7add11 A9 Am9 D9 Am9 C9
You can't keep your seat! *Spoken:* Professor! Start your beat!
mf

G
Come a - long! Get in it! You'll love the syn - co - pa - tion! The
G6
G♯dim
min - ute they be - gin it, You're shout - ing to the na - tion:
D
E♭
E
Dm7
Am7
D7
1. Gsus4 G
"Blow that Sweet And Low - Down!"
Em
Bm
Am9
D7
2. Gsus4
G
E♭9
G
Low - Down!"
p
sf
3

CONCERTO IN F

The notorious success of *Rhapsody in Blue,* incited primarily by the "jazz versus classical" debate, encouraged further commissions of "serious" Gershwin works, the second coming from no less august an organization than the New York Symphony Society through its conductor Walter Damrosch.

In July of 1925 Gershwin therefore began sketching what he called "New York Concerto." Some of this early work was done at Chautauqua, at a musical colony to which he had been invited by his friend, the great piano teacher, Ernest Hutcheson. The problem was that Gershwin's piano playing so captivated Hutcheson's piano students that they tended to invade the composer's cottage when he should have been working. Eventually the cottage in Chatauqua, N.Y. was placed off limits during part of the day so Gershwin could get some work done on the concerto.

Later he returned to his brownstone on 103rd Street in New York City to find that working in that crowded colony presented a similar problem (by this time it might be noted, he was also working on two musical scores—*Song of the Flame* and *Tip-Toes*—in addition to the concerto). To get away from the congested Gershwin household he finally rented a couple of rooms in a nearby hotel (the Whitehall on Broadway and 100th Street) in order to be able to concentrate on the concerto.

By September he completed the piano sketches and began the orchestration. Since there was more time to give to the concerto he would do the orchestration himself. The myth of the time was that Gershwin knew nothing about orchestration (after all, Grofé did the work on the *Rhapsody*). It was also intimated that upon accepting the commission Gershwin rushed out to buy a book to find out what a concerto was. (He did acquire a copy of Forsythe's *Orchestration,* a standard reference in the library of most musicians). While this is a characteristic anecdote, the truth was that Gershwin was quite familiar with orchestration, had studied it, in fact, as early as 1919 with Edward Kilenyi and later with Rossetter G. Cole at Columbia University. Of all his large works only the *Rhapsody in Blue* was orchestrated by another hand and that simply because of the time factor, not because Gershwin had been unable to do it (in fact, his piano score contains many suggestions as to instrumentation).

Despite distractions and interruptions Gershwin completed the *Concerto in F* (his final title) by November 10, 1925 in plenty of time for the performance at Carnegie Hall. It is unique among his compositions in that it is cast (more or less) in the strict classic form of the concerto—his creativity being more closely attuned to the freer rhapsodies, preludes and overtures. The concerto marked a long step forward for the young composer(he was twenty-seven), manifesting a mastery of form and orchestration that must have amazed those who regarded George Gershwin as a Tin Pan Alley upstart who had pushed his way into Carnegie Hall by sheer dint of nerve (the technical term, non-Freudian, is "chutzpa").

His more vociferous champions (he suffered from no paucity of these) were somewhat disappointed. The concerto was more conventional, not so outrageous as the rhapsody of the year before, it was not redolent—as some liked to think—of the bawdy house like the earlier work. And yet it was pure Gershwin, abounding in song-like themes, capricious rhythms and colorful orchestration. Performed for the first time on December 3, 1925, with the composer as soloist, the *Concerto in F* has remained in the active repertory of orchestras throughout the world and is undoubtedly the most played, best loved concerto for piano and orchestra written by an American.

George at work on the Concerto in F *in a N.Y. hotel (away from the family hubub).*

Ira and Lou Paley in dashing attire; Lou Paley supplied early lyrics to George's songs.

MAYBE

Lyrics by IRA GERSHWIN

Music by GEORGE GERSHWIN

F
Am7-5
D7-9
Gm
Cares will all dis - ap - pear.
Though hap - pi -
C9
Fmaj7
B♭
F
Fmaj7
Dm7
ness is late,
And we must
wait,
There's no need to be
G9
G7-5
C9
C7
ner - vous
There are dreams at your
ser - vice.
poco rit.
Refrain:
F
Gm7
C7
Gm7
C7
Soon or late,
May - be,
p
a tempo
con calore
L.H.
L.H.

F
F7
D
Gm
C7
Cm7
Gm
C7
If you wait,
May - be,
F
Dm6
E7
Some kind fate,
May - be,
p
Am
Dm6
E7
Am7
D7-9
Will help you dis - cov - er Where to find
p
molto gentile
Gm7
C7
F
your lov - er. You will hear
p

Gm7 C7 Gm7 C7 F F7 D
You - hoo, He'll be near
Gm C7 Cm7 Gm C7 F F7
you - hoo. Par - a - dise will o - pen its gate
mf molto cresc.
B♭ G7 F Fdim C7
May - be soon, May - be
p
1. F Dm Gm7 C7
late.
mf
2. F D♭7 F
late.
poco smorzando
Ped. *

CLAP YO' HANDS

Lyrics by IRA GERSHWIN

Music by GEORGE GERSHWIN

Dm
A+5
Dm7
G
Dm7
G
A7+5
Noth - in' but trou - ble if he has found, If he has found you,
p
Dm
B♭7
Gm7
C7
chil - dren, But you can chase the Hoo - doo with the dance that
F
Dm6
Am
E7
you do. Let me lead the
mf marcato
mp
Am
Fdim
A
E7
A
A7
way; Ju - bi - lee to - day.

Dm A+5 Dm7 G A7+5 Dm G7 C7
He'll nev - er hound you, Stamp on the ground, you chil - dren! Come on!
p
Refrain:
F C7 F
Clap - a yo' hand! Slap - a yo' thigh! Hal - le - lu - yah! Hal - le -
p-f
C7 F7 Bb Bb7 Bb6 Dbm6 C7
lu - yah! Ev - 'ry - bod - y come a - long and join the ju - bi -
F Bbm6 F
lee! Clap - a yo' hand!
mf

C7
F
C7
F7
Slap-a yo' thigh! Don't you lose time, don't you lose time, Come a-long, it's
B♭
B♭7
B♭6
D♭m6
C7
F
shake yo' shoes time now for you and me!
G7
C
Fm
F
Fm
On the sands of time you are on-ly a
C
C7
Fmaj7
B♭
peb-ble; Re-mem-ber, trou-ble must be

Bbm C+5 C7+5 Fm C7
treat - ed just like a reb - el,
Send him to the deb - ble!
F C7 F
Clap - a yo' hand! Slap - a yo' thigh! Hal - le - lu - yah! Hal - le -
C7 F7 Bb Bb7 C7
la - yah! Ev - 'ry-bod - y come a - long and join the ju - bi -
1. F Db7 C7
lee.
2. F Bb F
lee.

DO-DO-DO

Lyrics by IRA GERSHWIN

Music by GEORGE GERSHWIN

Fm7 Bb7 Eb Gm7 C7
Kay: I re - mem - ber it quite, 'Twas a won - der - ful night!
Jimmy: I can't see that at all True love nev - er should pall.
poco cresc.
Bb G7-9 G7 C7 F7 Bb Bbdim Fm7 Bb7 Bb7+5
Jimmy: Oh, how I'd a - dore it, If you would en - core it. Oh,
Kay: I was on - ly teas - ing What you did was pleas - ing. Oh,
mf
p
un poco rit.
Refrain:
Eb6 C9 Cm7 F7
Do, Do, Do what you've done, done, done be - fore,
p - f a tempo
Bb7 Bb7+5 Eb6 C9
ba - by. Do, Do, Do what I Do, Do, Do a -

Cm7 F7 Bb7 Bb7+5 Eb Bb6 Cm Gm
dore, ba - by. Let's try a - gain, Sigh a - gain,
poco espressivo
Ab Fm7 Bb7 Eb F Bb Gm Cm F7
Fly a - gain to heav - en. Ba - by, see, It's A, B, C,
mf
Bb Abm6 Bb7+5 Eb6
I love you and you love me. I know, know, know what a
Jimmy: You, dear, dear, dear lit - tle
deciso
p
C9 Cm7 F7 Bb7 Bb7+5
beau, beau, beau should do, ba - by. So
dear, dear, dear come here snap - py And

Eb6 Eb7 Abmaj7
don't, don't, don't say it won't, won't, won't come true,
see, see, see lit - tle me, me, me make you
Fm7-5 Bb+5 Eb Gm Cm Ebmaj7 Ab C7+5
ba - by. My heart be - gins to hum: Dum - de-dum - de-
hap - py. Kay: My heart be - gins to sigh Di - de-di - de-
mf
Fm Abm6 Bb7 Bb7+5 Eb6 C7 Fm7 Bb7
dum - dum - dum, So Do, Do, Do what you've done, done, done be -
di - di - di So Do, Do, Do what you've done, done, done be -
p
1. Eb Cb Bb7
fore. Oh,
2. Eb Cb Bb7 Eb
fore.
mf
mf
3
sf

SOMEONE TO WATCH OVER ME

Lyrics by IRA GERSHWIN
French Lyrics by EMILIA RENAUD
Music by GEORGE GERSHWIN

Eb Bb11 Edim Fm7-5 Bb7 Eb Ebmaj7
had in mind. Look - ing ev - 'ry - where, Have-n't
dans l'i - dée, Re - gar - dant par - tout sans le
Eb9 Eb7 Abmaj7 Cm F7
found him yet; He's the big af - fair I can - not for - get.
ren - con - trer; C'est un gars que je ne puis ou - bli - er.
Fm7 Gm Bb7 Eb Ab
On - ly man I ev - er think of with re - gret.
Le seul homme à qui je pense a - vec re - gret.
Eb D7-9 Gm C Gm
I'd like to add his in - i - tial to my mon - o - gram.
Mon nom pour ses i - ni - tia - les, je le chan - ge - rais.
mp

C7
Bb
Bb6
Cm7
F7
Bb
Ab
Gm
Bb7
Tell me, where is the shep-herd for this lost lamb.
Pour la bre - bis per-due, où est le ber - ger?
mf
un poco rall.
Refrain:
Eb
Eb7
Ab6
Abdim
Eb
Ebdim
There's a some-bod-y I'm long-ing to see. I hope that he
Il est un quel-qu'un que je veux re - voir Cha - que ma - tin
p a tempo
Bb7
Bbdim
Fm
C7
Fm
Am7-5
Bb11 Bb7
Eb
G7+5
Turns out to be Some - one who'll watch o - ver me.
et cha - que soir, Et qui me pro - té - ge - ra.
Abmaj7
Bb7
Eb
Eb7
Ab6
Abdim
I'm a lit - tle lamb who's lost in the wood;
Je suis la bre - bis per - due dans le bois;
p

Eb Ebdim Bb7 Bbdim Fm C7 Fm
I know I could Al - ways be good To one who'll
Je don - ne - rai Tou - te ma foi A qui me
mf
Am7-5 Bb11 Bb7 Eb Eb7 Ab Bb7 Eb
watch o - ver me. Al - though he
pro - tê - ge - ra. Quoi - qu'il ne
Ab
may not be the man some Girls think of as
soit pas un hom - me pos - sé - dant gran - de
Eb D7 D7+5 D7 G7
hand - some. To my heart he car - ries the
beau - té De mon coeur il por - te la

C C7 F7 Bb7 Eb Eb7
key. Won't you tell him please to
clef. Qu'on lui di - se donc de
p
Ab6 Abdim Eb Ebdim Bb7 Bbdim
put on some speed, Fol - low my lead, Oh, how I need
bien se hâ - ter J'ai tant be - soin De ce quel - qu'un,
Fm C7 Fm Bb11 Am7-5 Bb7
1. Eb Eb7 Ab G7+5
Some - one To Watch O - ver Me.
Quel - qu'un pour me pro - té - ger.
mf
Fm7 Bb7+5
2. Eb Eb7 Ab Abm Eb
Me.
ger.
mf
Ped. *

PRELUDES FOR PIANO

The *Preludes* were composed for a recital by the Peruvian (though born in Liverpool) contralto, Marguerite d'Alvarez. This was a patent sequel to the Gauthier program of 1923, except that by December 4, 1926, when the first so-called "Futurist" program took place at the Roosevelt Hotel in Manhattan, the name of Gershwin meant something in the larger world of music. The program, besides the song by D'Alvarez, featured a two-piano rendition of the *Rhapsody in Blue* (already a trademark) and the *Preludes* presented solo by the composer.

Practically from the beginning of his musical career George Gershwin began the practice of preserving musical ideas in notebooks ("iceboxes", he called them) upon which he could draw when the need arose for a theme or rhythmic idea. Most of these were readily expanded into songs; a number specifically intended for piano he called "novelettes". It was from these that the *Preludes* were drawn for the d'Alvarez recitals, five being performed in New York and six on January 16, 1927 in Boston.

These engaging miniatures reveal Gershwin at his most sensitive, reflective (especially true of the second prelude) and imaginative. He chose, however, not to publish all of those he had played; instead he formed a balanced suite of three, two rhythmic pieces enclosing a haunting metropolitan blues. As for the other preludes, two were probably combined into a violin and piano piece, *Short Story* (undoubtedly Gershwin's least-known work) and another remains in manuscript. The three published *Preludes for Piano* are good Gershwin indeed; in them he worked with those forms of which he was an undoubted master—song and dance.

FUNNY FACE

Lyrics by IRA GERSHWIN

Music by GEORGE GERSHWIN

Gm Gm6 Cm7-5 Bb F9 F6
peals to me, Please, don't think I've sud - den - ly gone
Cit - y, dear, Miss A - mer - i - ca I'd nev - er
Bb Bb (Abbass) Gb Db7 Gb
mad. You have all the qual - i - ties of Pe - ter Pan,
be. Truth to tell, though, you're not such a lot your - self,
Db7 Gb Bb7 Ab Bb7 Eb
I'd go far be - fore I'd find a sweet - er pan.
As a Paul Swan you are not so hot your - self. And yet
Refrain:
F9 Bb7 F9 Bb9 F9 Bb7 Bb9+5
I love your Fun - ny Face, Your
I love your Fun - ny Face, Your
p - mf

Eb Ab7 Eb Cm7
sun - ny Fun - ny Face, For
sun - ny Fun - ny Face. You
F7 Cm7 F7 Fm7 Bb7 Bb+5
you're a cu - tie With more than beau - ty, You've
can't re - pair it, So I de - clare it is
Eb6 Cm6 Bb9+5 Gm7-5 C9 F9
got a lot Of per - son - al - i - ty N. T. A.,
quite all right Jimmy: Like Ron - ald Col - man? So's your ol' man!
Frankie:
dolce
Bb7 F9 Bb7 F9 Bb7 Bb9+5
Thou - sand laughs I've found, In
Yet it's ver - y clear, I'm

Eb7
Bb9
Eb7
Ab7
hav - ing you a - round.
glad when you are near.
Ebmaj7
Bb9
Eb9
Though you're no Glo - ria Swan - son, For
Though you're no hand - some Har - ry, For
Abmaj7
Cm7
F7
Bb7
F9
Bb7
Bb9+5
worlds I'd not re - place your sun - ny Fun - ny
worlds I'd not re - place your sun - ny Fun - ny
1.
Eb
Cb9
Abm6
Eb
Cb7
Fm7
F9
2.
Eb
Abm6
Eb
Ab9
Eb
Face. I Face.
f
p
dim.

'S WONDERFUL

Lyrics by IRA GERSHWIN

Music by GEORGE GERSHWIN

Cm Eb Am7-5 D7 Gm Bb7+5 Gm7-5 C7
How can words ex - press Your di - vine ap - peal?
When you said you care, 'Mag - ine my e - mosh;
Fm C Fm7-5 Bb7 Eb Bb Edim C7
You can nev - er guess All the love I feel.
I swore then and there Per - ma - nent de - vosh.
Bb F9 F7 Bb Dbm6 Gb7
From now on, la - dy, I in - sist,
You made all oth - er boys seem blah;
Bb F9 F7 Fm7(Bb bass) Abm Bb7
For me no oth - er girls ex - ist.
Just you a - lone filled me with Aah!
un poco rit.

Refrain:

Eb Eb6 Eb Eb6 C7 C#dim C7 C#dim
'S won - der-ful! 'S mar - ve-lous!
p - mf a tempo
Fm11 Bb6 Bb7 Eb6 Eb Eb6 Eb Eb Eb6
You should care for me! 'S aw - ful nice!
Eb Eb6 C7 C#dim C7 C#dim Fm11 Bb6 Bb7
'S par - a-dise! 'S what I love to
Eb6 Am7-5 G D7
see! You've made my life so
My dear, it's four-leaf
mf

G D7 Dm6 C9
glam - o - rous, You can't blame me for feel - ing
clo - ver time, From now on my heart's work-ing
cresc.
F7 Bb9 Bb7-9 Eb Eb6 Eb Eb6
a - mor-ous!
o - ver -time!
Oh! 'S won - der-ful!
p
Cm F9 Cm F Fm7 Edim Fm7 Bb7
'S mar - vel - ous! That you should care for
mf
p
1. Eb Gm Fm Ab Gm Cm Fm7 Bb
me!
2. Eb Abmaj7 Ab6 Eb
me!
mf
mf

HE LOVES AND SHE LOVES

Lyrics by IRA GERSHWIN

Music by GEORGE GERSHWIN

Abmaj9 Ab6 Abmaj7 Ab7 C(Gbass) F7-5
full of hap-py fac - es, It's be-cause they
Em7 C Dm7 G7 C D7 Gm7 C7
all love That won-drous thing they call love.
rall. e dim.
Slowly (with sentiment)
Refrain:
F C7 Am7-5
He Loves And She Loves and they love, So
p - mf
D+5 D(Cbass) Bb6 Bbm C6 C(Bbbass) F(Abass) Dm
why can't you love and I love too?
scherzando

Gm7 C7 F C7 Am7-5
Birds love and bees love and whis-per - ing
D+5 D(Cbass) B♭6 B♭m C6 C7 F Dm6 B♭7
trees love, And that's what we both should do.
Am7 A♭dim Gm7 C7 F7 Cm7 F6 F9
Oh, I al - ways knew, some day
B♭ F7 B♭ D7
you'd come a - long; We'll make a

Am7-5 D+5 D7 Gm Gm7 C9 Gm7 C7
two - some that just can't go wrong, hear me:
rit.
F C7 Am7-5
He Loves And She Loves and they love, So
a tempo
D+5 D(Cbass) Bb6 Bbm C6 C7
won't you love me as I love
why can't you love and I love,
1. F F+5 Bb Gm7 C6 C7
you.
2. F F+5 F
too?
f

MY ONE AND ONLY

Lyrics by IRA GERSHWIN
Music by GEORGE GERSHWIN

F Bb9 F Bm7-5 E7
I more than mere - ly love you sin - cere - ly,
Though we're not strang - ers, you see the dan - gers
Am Am6 C E+5 Am F#dim
My cards are on the ta - ble.
Of tak - ing me for grant - ed.
C7 No chord F F+5 F6 F#dim
There must be lots of oth - er men you hyp - no - tize.
And if you cared you should have told me long a - go;
C7 No chord F Gb G F7
All of a sud - den I've be - gun to re - al - ize as fol - lows:
Dear, oth - er wise how in the world was I to know? Jim: Oh, lis - ten:
rall.

Refrain:
Cm7-5
F7
Cm7-5
Jimmy: My One And On - ly, What am I gon-na do if you
p - mf a tempo
F7
Cm7-5
Eb7
F7
Bb
turn me down, When I'm so cra - zy o - ver you?
espressivo
mf
Bbm
Cm7-5
F7
Cm7-5
I'd be so lone - ly, Where am I gon-na go if you
p
F7
Cm7-5
Eb7
F7
Bb
turn me down? Why black-en all my skies of blue?
espressivo

F Bb F7 Bb Bbmaj7 Bb7+5
I tell you I'm not ask - ing an - y mi - ra - cle;
mf
Eb9 Ebm Bb Bbmaj7
It can be done! It can be done! I know a cler - gy - man who
Bb7+5 Eb9 Gb9 F7+5 F7
will grow ly - ri - cal And make us one, and make us one. So

Cm7-5
F7
Cm7-5
My One And On - ly, There is-n't a rea-son why you should
3
p

F7
Cm7-5
E♭7
F7
turn me down
When I'm so cra - zy o-ver
espressivo

1.
B♭
G7
F7
2.
B♭
E♭m
B♭
you!
you!
mf
mf
sf

THE BABBITT AND THE BROMIDE

Lyrics by IRA GERSHWIN

Music by GEORGE GERSHWIN

(D)
F#7
They both were sol - id cit - i - zens, they
That they had both de - vel - oped in ten
A harp each one was car - ry - ing and
p
3
Eb7
F#7
both had been a - round, And as they spoke you clear- ly saw their
years, there was no doubt, And so, of course, they had an aw - ful
both were wear-ing wings, And this is what they said as they were
A7
(D)
D7
feet were on the ground.
lot to talk a - bout;
strum-ming on the strings;
ff
sffz

Refrain:
G D7 G C G C
1.
2. "Hel - lo! How are you? How - za folks? What's
3.
p
p - mf
G C D7 C D7 D6 D7
new? I'm great! That's good! Ha - ha! Knock
sempre stacc.
G D7 G D7 G C G C
wood! Well, well! What say? How - ya been? Nice
G C D7 C D7 D6 D7
day. How's tricks? What's new? That's fine! How are

G
B7
you?
Nice weath - er we are hav - ing, but it
I'm sure I know your face, but I just
You've grown a lit - tle stout - er since I

Em
B7
gives me such a pain; I've tak - en my um -
can't re - call your name, Well, how've you been, old
saw you last, I think; You must come o - ver

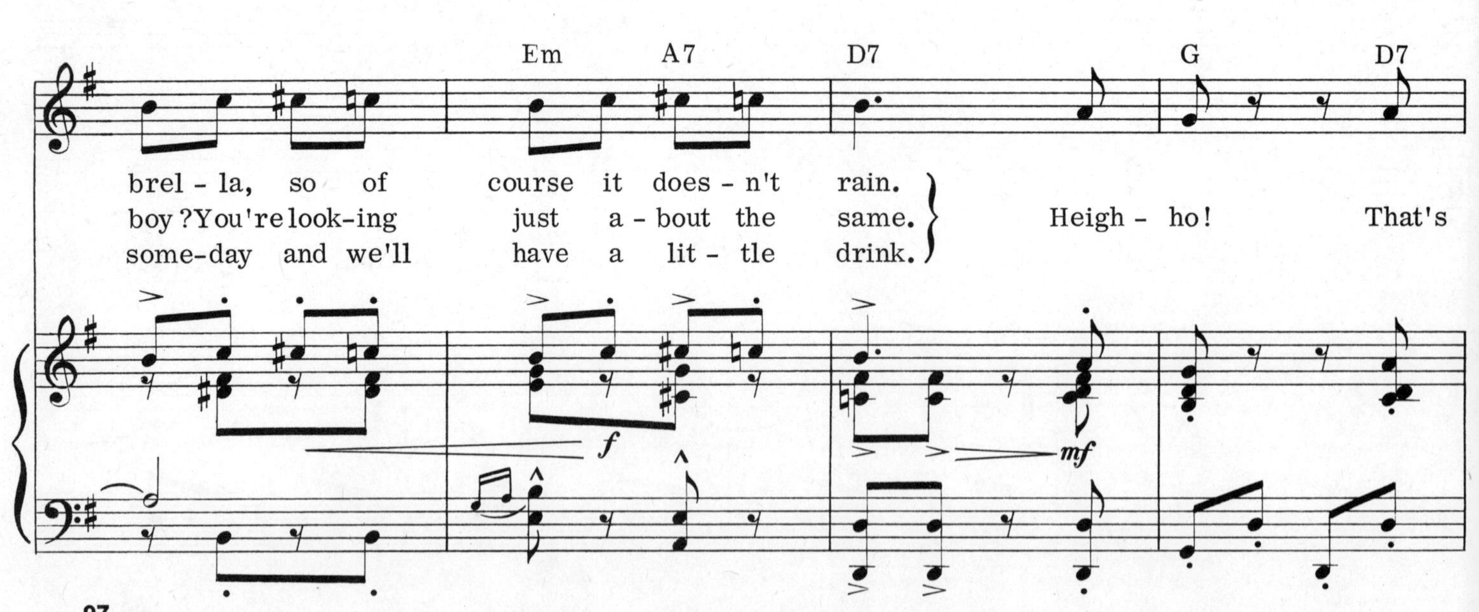
Em
A7
D7
G
D7
brel - la, so of course it does - n't rain.
boy? You're look-ing just a - bout the same.
some-day and we'll have a lit - tle drink.
Heigh - ho! That's
f
mf

G C G C G C D7 C
life! What's new? How-za wife? Got to run! Oh,
D7 D6 D7 G C
my! Ta - ta! Ol-ive oil! Good - bye!
Dance:
fz
G D7 G D7
marcato
1.2.
G B7 Em D. S. 3. G
sf
ff
D. S.
sf

I'VE GOT A CRUSH ON YOU

Lyrics by IRA GERSHWIN

Music by GEORGE GERSHWIN

Eb Bb D A7 D
wore down my re-sis-tance; I fell, and it was swell.
Cm7 F7 Bb Bbdim Cm7 F7 Bb6 Cm7 F7
Ann: You're my big and brave and hand-some Ro-me-o. How I
Bb Bb(A bass) Gm7 C7 F7 Bb Eb Bb
won you I shall nev-er, nev-er know. Timothy: It's not that you're at-trac-tive, But
Eb Gm7 C7 F9 Ebm6 F7
oh, my heart grew ac-tive When you came in-to view.

Refrain:
Tacet
B♭maj7
B♭dim
Cm7
F11
F7
I've Got A Crush On You, sweet-ie pie,
p - mf
All the day and night-time hear me sigh. I
B♭
Gm7
C9
B7
C7
nev - er had the least no - tion that I could
fall with so much e - mo - tion. Could you coo?

Cm7 F11 F7 B♭maj7 B♭dim
Could you care For a cun-ning cot-tage
Cm7 D7+5 D7 Gm7 Am Gm7 C9
we could share? The world will par - don my
B♭maj7 B♭6 C9 A6 F7
mush, 'Cause I've got a crush, my ba - by, on
1. B♭ Em7-5 F7sus F7
you. I've Got A
2. B♭ Gm6 F7 B♭
you.
fz
mf
mf
fz

AN AMERICAN IN PARIS

An American in Paris is Gershwin's first composition for orchestra alone, the first without a brilliant piano part for himself; it did serve, however, as a vehicle when he decided to try his hand at conducting.

Its origin dates to a 1926 visit to Paris (not the more publicized one of 1928). He had called on his friends, Mabel and Robert Schirmer and during a walk had become taken with the musical possibilities of the famed French taxi-horns. Accompanied one day by Mabel Schirmer he shopped along the Avenue de la Grand Armée and acquired a set of four of these horns. When it came time to leave, he autographed a photo of himself for the Schirmers identifying himself as "An American in Paris."

He had already composed the opening "walking theme"—into which the taxi-horns were worked—as a dance for Fred Astaire. Since it hadn't been used in a musical, Gershwin—with characteristic frugality—appropriated it for the new orchestral piece. It is certainly one of his most inspired inventions.

The idea had to be set aside for a time as he devoted himself to the scores of no less than three shows (the first version of *Strike Up the Band, Funny Face* and *Rosalie)* during 1927-28. In March of 1928, then, the Gershwins were ready for a rest and a trip abroad and, like so many other Americans of the time, set out for Paris. Ira, sister Frances, and Ira's wife Leonore, were determined to be tourists; George, for his part, brought the sketches of a new work with him and was equally determined to become a pupil of either Nadia Boulanger or Maurice Ravel (the latter was an ardent Gershwin fan). When they both rejected him, giving as a reason that his musical equipment was fine the way it was, he had plenty of time for the new piece and even for some sightseeing. There were also concerts (where to his delight he heard much Gershwin), parties (ditto, much provided by himself), musicales (more ditto) and other social activities.

Meanwhile, since he loved the excitement and bustle, he had no trouble working on the new composition, which he referred to as "a tone poem for orchestra." The lovely blues theme was written in the Hotel Majestic in Paris. Since Gershwin all but worked in public, word had gotten out that a new concert piece was being created and people (mostly musician friends) flocked to the Majestic to hear it in progress. Walter Damrosch, also vacationing in Europe at the time, got word and cabled to reserve its first performance for the New York Philharmonic-Symphonic Society. Gershwin agreed (though the work was not yet complete) and continued to enjoy his Paris stay as well as making a side trip to Vienna (meeting waltz kings Franz Lehar and Emmerich Kalman). He was welcomed everywhere—he could hardly enter a cafe without the orchestra bursting into the strains of *Rhapsody in Blue.*

After four months of this, the time came to return to New York; work was about to begin on a new Gertrude Lawrence musical, *Treasure Girl.* Characteristically, Gershwin threw himself into the routine with verve, working on one project then the other. In August of 1928 he began orchestrating from the completed piano sketch of the *American,* finishing that chore on November 18 (*Treasure Girl* had opened ten days before), in plenty of time for the Carnegie Hall premiere on December 13.

Before the concert Gershwin made some observations on the work that might be better known.

"This new piece, really a rhapsodic ballet, is written very freely and is the most modern music I've attempted. . . . My purpose here is to portray the impressions of an American visitor in Paris, as he strolls about the city and listens to various street noises and absorbs the French atmosphere.

"As in my other orchestral compositions I've not endeavored to represent any definite scenes in this music. The rhapsody is programmatic only in a general impressionistic way, so that the individual listener can read into the music as much as his imagination pictures for him.

"The opening gay section is followed by a rich blues with a strong rhythmic under-current. Our American friend perhaps after strolling into a café and having a couple of drinks, has succumbed to a spasm of homesickness. The harmony here is both more intense and simple than in the preceding pages. This blues rises to a climax followed by a coda in which the spirit of the music returns to the vivacity and bubbling exuberance of the opening part with its impressions of Paris. Apparently the homesick American, having left the café and reached the open air, has disowned his spell of the blues and once again is an alert spectator of Parisian life. At the conclusion the street noises and French atmosphere are triumphant."

George with the French taxi-horns he brought back from Paris. At right, famed tenor Richard Crooks considers the new orchestral instrument with some doubt.

George in Europe during his 1928 trip which produced An American in Paris.

LIZA

Lyrics by IRA GERSHWIN & GUS KAHN

Music by GEORGE GERSHWIN

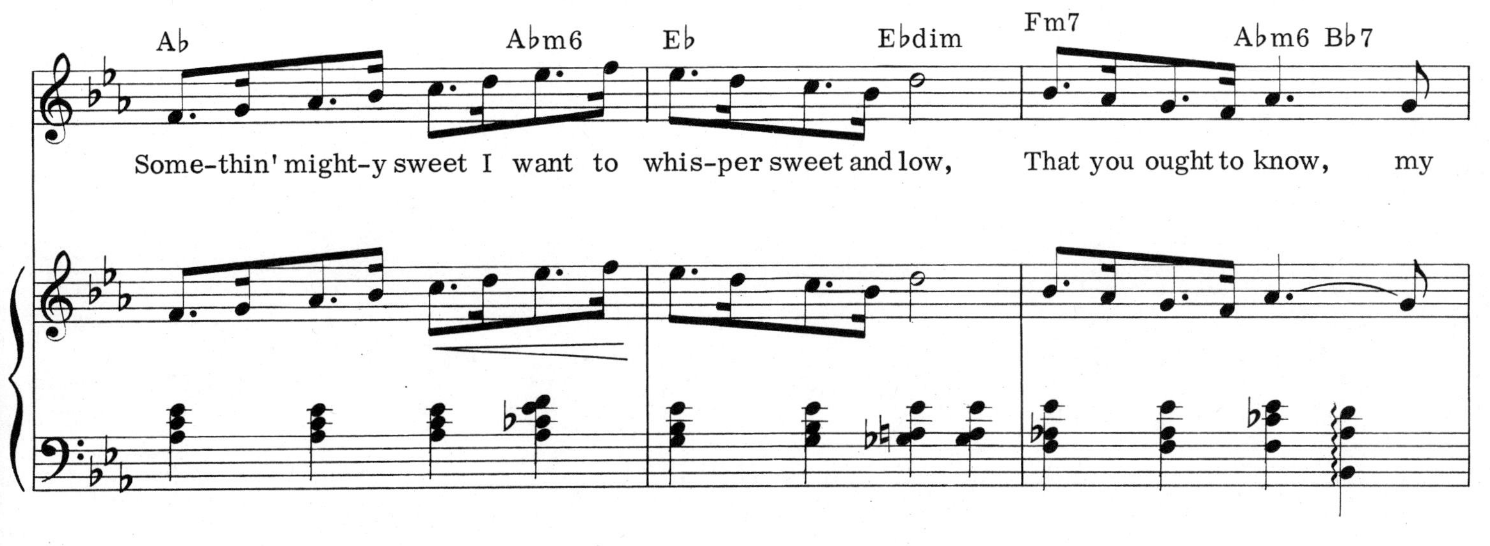
Ab
Abm6
Eb
Ebdim
Fm7
Abm6 Bb7
Some-thin' might-y sweet I want to whis-per sweet and low, That you ought to know, my

Gm7
C7
Ab6
Abm6
Eb
F7-9
Li - za! I get lone-some, hon - ey, when I'm all a-lone so long;

Bb
Eb Ebm
Bb
C7 Ebm6
Bb Gm7 Cm7 F9
Bb Fm7 Gm Bb7
Don't make me wait; Don't hes - i - tate; Come and hear my song:
rall.

Refrain:
Eb Bb7 Cdim C7 Abm6 Cdim Bbm6 Eb9
Li - za, Li - za, skies are gray,
p - mf a tempo
Ab Fm7 Gm C9 Fm Bb7
But if you'll smile on me All the clouds-'ll roll a -
Eb Ab Eb Fm7 Eb Bb7 Cdim C7 Abm6 Cdim
way. Li - za, Li - za, don't de -
Bbm6 Eb9 Ab Fm7 Gm C9 Fm Bb7
lay, Come, keep me com - pa - ny, And the clouds-'ll roll a-

Eb G7+5 G7 Cm Cm7 Cdim G7+5 G7 Cm
way. See the hon-ey-moon a - shin - in'
mf
Gdim Eb7 Ab Fm Bbm7 Eb7 Ab6 Ab Ab9 Bb7
down; We should make a date with Par - son Brown. So,
fp
Eb Bb7 Cdim C7 Abm6 Cdim Bbm6 Eb9 Ab Fm7
Li - za, Li - za, name the day When you be -
Gm C9 Fm Bb7
long to me And the clouds-'ll roll a - way.
1. Eb Db Bm7 Bb7
2. Eb
way.

SOON

Lyrics by IRA GERSHWIN

Music by GEORGE GERSHWIN

Eb m6 F9 Bb F7 Gm Dm
fast. The man - y lone - ly nights and days when this duf - fer
Eb Bb C7 Bb
just had to suf - fer, are past. Joan: Life will be a
F9-5 F9 Bb Bb7 Bb7+5
dream song, Love will be the theme song.
poco rit.
Refrain: Not fast with tender expression
Eb Eb m6 Bb m6
Jim: Soon the lone - ly nights will be
Joan: Soon, my dear, you'll nev - er be
p-f

C7+5 C7 Fm C7 A♭m6
end - ed. Soon, two hearts as one will be
lone - ly. Soon, you'll find I live for you
B♭7+5 B♭7 E♭ B♭7 E♭ E♭7 Cm E♭7+5 A♭6
blend - ed. I've found the hap - pi - ness I've wait - ed for;
on - ly. When I'm with you who cares what time it is,
L.H.
poco rit.
a tempo
Fm C7 Fm Fm6 G7 Cm7
The on - ly girl that I was fat - ed for.
Or what the place or what the cli - mate is?
poco rit.
a tempo
Fm7 B♭7 E♭ E♭m6 B♭m6
Oh! Soon a lit - tle cot - tage will
Oh! Soon our lit - tle ship will come
mp

C7+5 C7 Fm C7+5 Abm6
find us safe with all our cares far be-
sail - ing home through ev - 'ry storm, nev - er
Bb7+5 Bb7 Eb Bb7 Eb Eb7 Eb7+5
hind us. The day you're mine this world will
fail - ing. The day you're mine this world will
L.H.
poco rit.
Ab Abm6 Eb Cm7 Ab6 Bb7
be in tune: Let's make that day come
be in tune: Let's make that day come
mf
a tempo
p
1. Eb B7 Bb7
Soon.
2. Eb
Soon.
3
mf
dim.

STRIKE UP THE BAND

Lyrics by IRA GERSHWIN

Music by GEORGE GERSHWIN

Ab Bbm Fm C7 Fm C7 F C7
oth - er war, But if we are forced in - to one, The flag that we'll be
F Bb F C7 F F7 Bbm Ebm Bbm Ebm
fight - ing for, Is the Red and White and Blue One! We do not fa - vor
molto marcato
Bb7 Ebm Bbm Ebm6 Bbm Fm C7-5 F7 Bbm Ebm Bbm
war a - larms, Rum - ta - ta-tum - tum - tum! But if we hear the
rall.
Ebm6 Bbm Eb9 Bbm Fm Gbmaj7 F
call to arms, Rum-ta - ta-tum-tum, Rum-ta - ta-tum-tum, Rum-ta- ta-tum-tum - tum!

Refrain: *very marked*
F7 Bb Bb6 Bb Bdim
Let the drums roll out! Let the trum-pet call!
Spoken: (Boom boom boom) *Imitation of Trpt.:* (Ta - ta -
mf-f
ra - ta - ta - ta - ta!)
F7
While the peo - ple shout! Strike Up The
Shouted: (Hoo - ray!)
Bb Ab Bb7 Eb Eb6
Band! Hear the cym - bals ring!
Eb Edim
Call - ing one and all To the
Spoken: (Tszing-tszing-tszing!) *Trpt.:* (Ta - ta - ra - ta - ta - ta - ta!)

Bb7
Eb
mar - tial swing
Strike Up The Band!
Shouted: (Left, right!)
Ebm6 Bb Bb6 Bb Eb Ebmaj7
There is work to be done, to be done! There's a
Yank - ee Doo, Doo - dle - oo, Doo - dle - oo, We'll come
Am D9 Am D7 Gm C9
war to be won, to be won! Come, you son of a son of a
through, Doo - dle - oo, Doo - dle - oo, For the red, white and blue, Doo - dle -
Gm C7 F7 Eb F Gm F7 Bb Cm F7
gun! Take your stand! Fall in
oo, Lend a hand! With our

B♭ B♭6 Dm7 G9
line, yea bo! Come a - long, let's go!
flag un - furled, For a brave, new world!

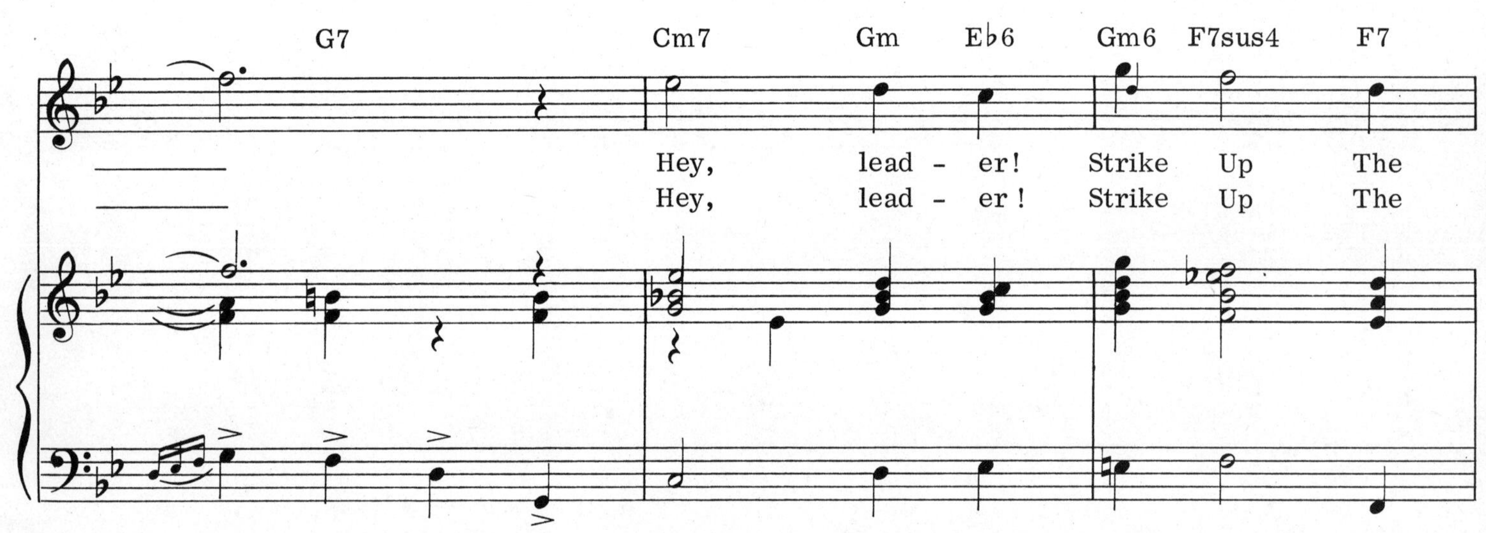
G7 Cm7 Gm E♭6 Gm6 F7sus4 F7
Hey, lead - er! Strike Up The
Hey, lead - er! Strike Up The

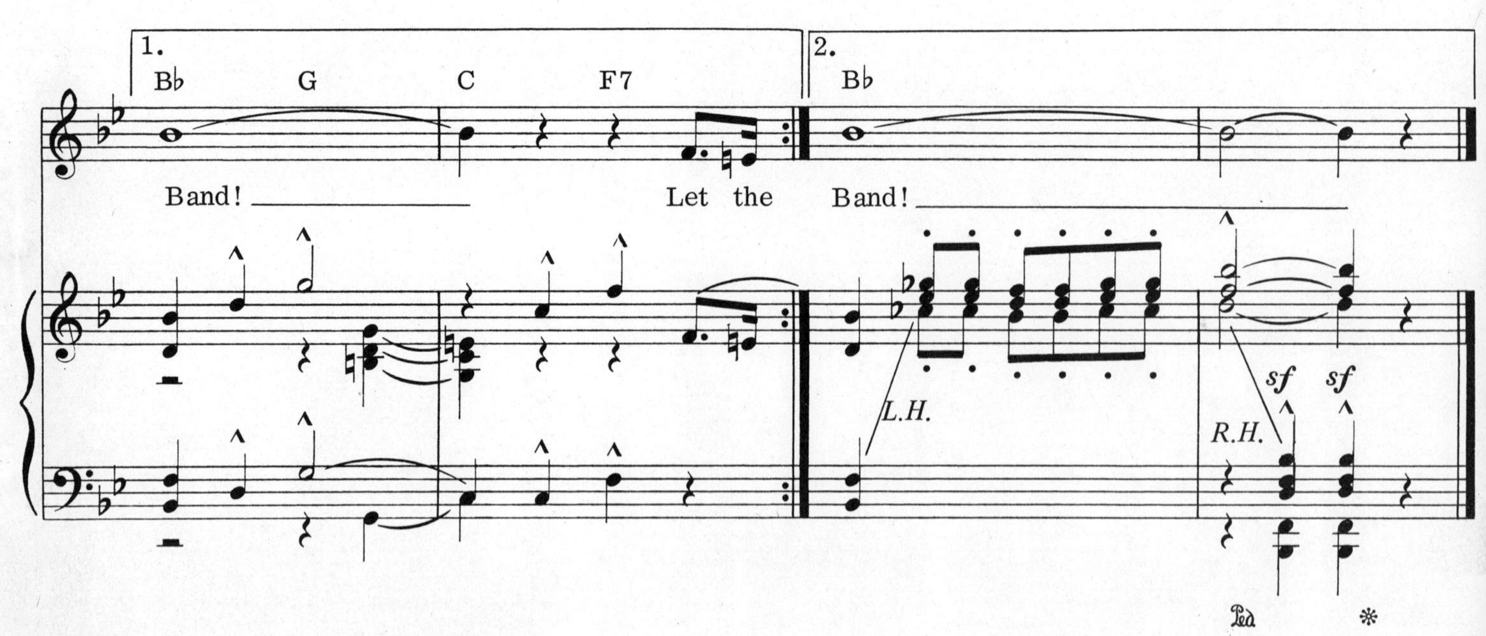
1.
B♭ G C F7
Band! Let the
2.
B♭
Band!
L.H.
R.H.
sf sf

Rehearsing with the Los Angeles Philharmonic (1937).

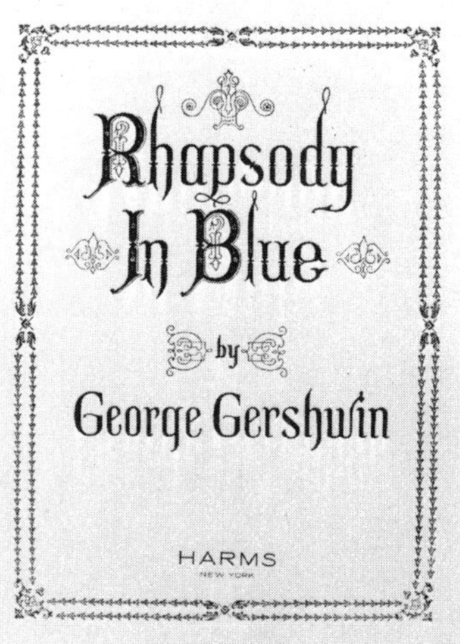

George with a friend (1930).

Ira, George and Buy Bolton, working on the Gershwin's first film, Delicious *(1931)*.

George, with actress Florence Rice, at the penthouse at 33 Riverside Drive, New York (1932).

BIDIN' MY TIME

Lyrics by IRA GERSHWIN

Music by GEORGE GERSHWIN

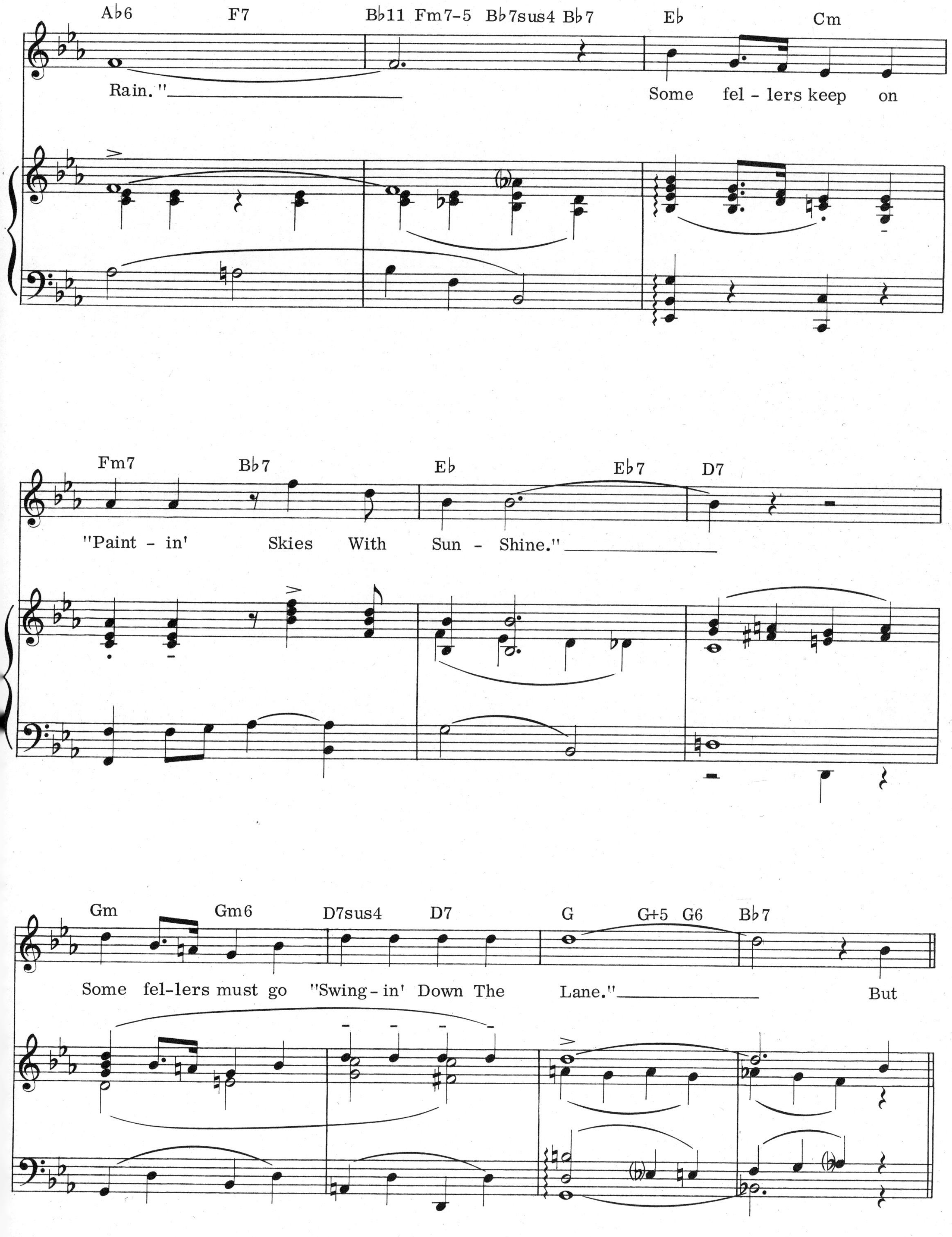

Ab6 F7 Bb11 Fm7-5 Bb7sus4 Bb7 Eb Cm

Rain." Some fel - lers keep on

Fm7 Bb7 Eb Eb7 D7

"Paint - in' Skies With Sun - Shine."

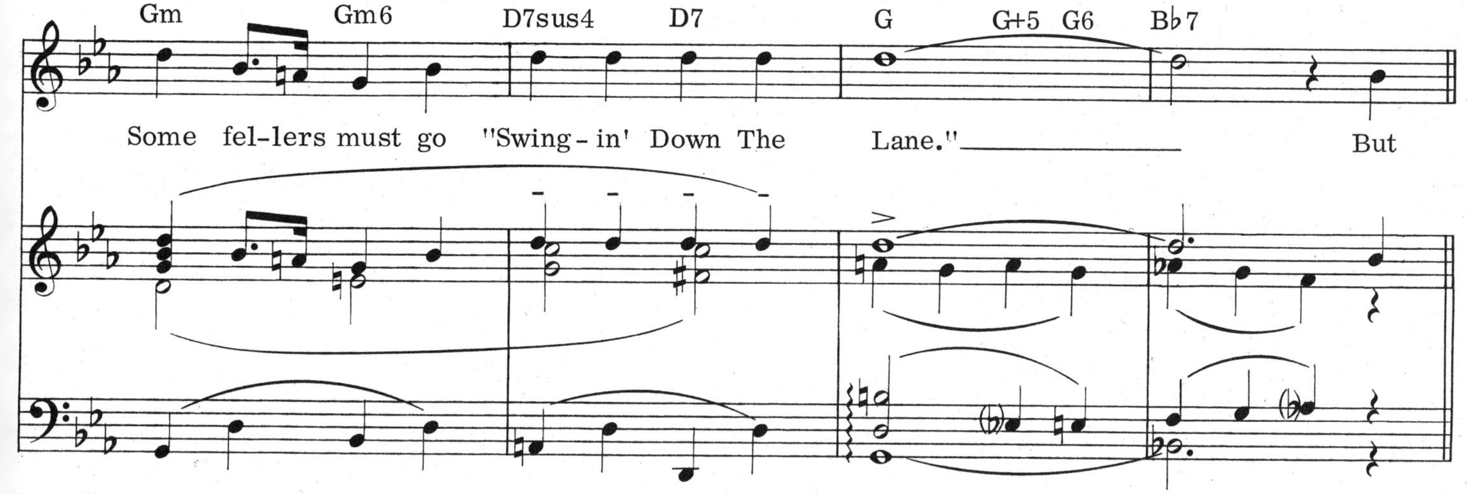

Refrain:
Eb Ab Fm7 Bb7sus4 Bb7 Eb Ab
I'm Bid-in' My Time; 'Cause that's the kind-a guy
I'm Bid-in' My Time; 'Cause that's the kind-a guy
p-mf
Fm7 Bb7sus4 Bb7 Eb C7 Fm7 Abm (F bass)
I'm, While oth-er folks grow diz-zy I keep bus-y
I'm. Be-gin-nin' on a Mon-day right through Sun-day,
Eb Bb7 Eb G7 C
Bid-in' My Time. Next year,
Bid-in' My Time. Give me,
mp
G7 C G7 F C
next year, Some-thin's bound to hap-pen;
give me Glass that's full of tin-kle,

Bb7 Eb Bb7 Eb Ebm Cm7 (C bass) F6 F9
This year, this year, I'll just keep on
Let me, let me Dream like Rip Van
mf
Bb11 Bb7 Bb9 Eb Ab Fm7 Bb7sus4 Bb7
nap - pin', And Bid - in' My Time 'Cause
Win - kle. He bid - ed his time, And
p
Eb Ab Fm7 Bb7sus4 Bb7 Eb C7
that's the kind - a guy I'm. There's no re - gret - tin'.
like that Win - kle guy I'm. Chas - in' 'way flies,
Fm7 Abm Eb Bb7 1. Eb Bb7 2. Eb
When I'm set - tin' Bid - in' My Time.
How the day flies, Bid - in' My Time.
mf
sf

EMBRACEABLE YOU

Lyrics by IRA GERSHWIN

Music by GEORGE GERSHWIN

G C#m7 F#7
What was it that con - trolled me? What kept my love - life
Qu'est - ce qui m'a con - tro - lé? Et gar - dé mon a -
Quie - ro que tú me ex - pli - ques, Qué es lo que de - bo ha -
B C#m7 F#7 B
lean? My in - tu - i - tion told me You'd come
mour? Si ce n'est que la pen - sée De te
cer? Cuan - do yo quie - ro ver - te, No me
Am7 D7 G Em A9 Em A9
on the scene. La - dy, lis - ten to the rhy - thm of my
voir un jour. De mon cœur é - cou - tes les bat - te - ments
quie - res ver, Cuan - do no te a - bra - zo, quie - res que te a -
Em Em6 Em A7 Am D6 Am D6 Am D6 Am D7
heart - beat, And you'll get just what I mean.
ryth - més, Qui t'ap - pel - lent bien ai - mée.
bra - ze; ¡Qué ma - ne - ra de que - rer!
rall. e dim.

Refrain:
Rhythmically
G C♯dim D7 Cadd9 Fm6 D7
Em - brace me, My sweet Em - brace - a - ble You!
Un bai - ser, mon a - do - ra - ble pou - pée!
Te a - bra - zo con to - da mi de - vo - ción.
p-mf
Am F7 D7 G D7sus4 G
Em - brace me, You ir - re - place - a - ble you!
Un bai - ser, Ir - ré - sis - ti - ble beau - té!
Te a - bra - zo y en - tre - go mi co - ra - zón.
Em Em7 Em6 F♯7 Bm B+5 Bm7 E9
Just one look at you, my heart grew tip - sy in me;
Un re - gard de toi peut faire cha - vi - rer mon coeur,
Te - mo tan - to que no me co - rres - pon - de - rás,
D D♯dim Em7 F♯m7 G6 A7 D7
You and you a - lone bring out the gyp - sy in me!
Je sais que toi seu - le peut fai - re mon bon - heur!
Que mis an - sias nun - ca, nun - ca com - pren - de - rás.

G C♯dim D7 Cadd9 Fm6 D7
I love all the man - y charms a - bout you;
J'ai - me tout ce qui me par - le de toi;
Me a - bra - zas sin de - mos - trar e - mo - ción.
Am F7 D7 G7 G7sus4 B♭m6 G7 C
A - bove all I want my arms a - bout you.
En - core plus je te veux tout pres de moi.
Me be - sas con tan es - ca - sa i - lu - sión.
Don't be a
Ne sois pas
No sé si
Am6 B7 Em E♭+5 G Em6 G
naugh - ty ba - by, Come to pa - pa, Come to pa - pa, do!
si mé - chan - te, Viens mon chou-chou, viens mon chou-chou, viens!
de - bo a - mar - te, Pe - ro pa - ra de - mos - trar mi a - mor,
My sweet Em -
Mon a - do -
Te a - bra - za -
L.H.
Cm6 D6 D7
brace - a - ble
ra - ble pou -
ré por los
1. G E♭ A D7
You!
pée!
dos.
2. G
You!
pée!
dos.

I GOT RHYTHM

Lyrics by IRA GERSHWIN

Music by GEORGE GERSHWIN

Cm Gm6 Eb9 Gm Gm7
tree sing Their day-ful of song, Why should-n't
Cm9 F7 Bb Fm7 Bb Fm7 Bb D D7
we sing a-long? I'm chip-per
A7+5 D7 Cm7 Eb9 D D7
all the day, Hap-py with my lot. How do I
A7+5 D7 Cm7 F7 Edim Gb7 F7 Bbm6 Ddim F7
get that way? Look at what I've got:
sf
f

(with abandon)
Refrain:
B♭ B♭6 Cm7 F7 B♭6 Edim Cm7 F7
I Got Rhy - thm, I got mu - sic,
p - mf
B♭ B♭6 Cm7 F7 E♭m6 B♭ F7 B♭ C♯dim F7
I got my man Who could ask for an-y-thing more?
B♭ B♭6 Cm7 F7 B♭6 Edim Cm7 F7 B♭ B♭6
I got dai - sies In green pas - tures, I got
Cm7 F7 E♭m6 B♭ F7 B♭ D7 Am7
my man Who could ask for an-y-thing more? Old man

Fm6 D9 G D+5 G9 G7 C7 Gm7 E♭m6 C9
Trou-ble, I don't mind him, You won't find him
C7-5 F7 C7 F7 B♭ B♭6 Cm7 F7 B♭6 Edim
'Round my door. I got star-light, I got
Cm7 F7 B♭ B♭6 Cm7 F7 E♭m6 B♭ Fm
sweet dreams, I got my man Who could ask for an-y-thing
G7 C7 F7 1. B♭ A♭ G♭ D♭ 2. B♭
more, Who could ask for an-y-thing more? more?
sfz
8

BUT NOT FOR ME

Lyrics by IRA GERSHWIN

Music by GEORGE GERSHWIN

G D+5 Dm C+5 Eb+5 Bm Db+5 Am D7-9
Bea - trice Fair-fax, don't you dare Ev - er tell me he will care; I'm
L.H.
G6 D9 D7-9 G F# G Edim
cer - tain It's the fi - nal cur - tain, I nev - er want to
Fm7 Bb7 Ab Bb7 Cm6
hear from an - y cheer - ful Pol - ly - an - nas, Who tell you
Fm7 Bb7-9 Bb7 Eb6 Bb7 Eb Bb7
fate, Sup-plies a mate; It's all ba - na - nas! They're writ - ing
(He's knock - ing)

Refrain:
Rather slow (smoothly)
Eb Bb7 Eb6 Bb7 Eb Bb7 Eb Bb7 Eb Bb7
songs of love, But Not For Me. A luck - y
on a door, But Not For Me. He'll plan a
p - mf
F7 Bb7 Eb9 Eb7
star's a - bove, But Not For Me. With love to
two by four, But Not For Me. I know that
Eb+5 Ab Fm7 Cm Fm7 F#dim Eb Cm Bb7 Eb
lead the way, I've found more clouds of gray Than an - y
love's a game; I'm puz - zled, just the same, Was I the
Eb+5 Fm7 Fm6 F7-5 Bb7 Eb Bb7
Rus - sian play Could guar - an - tee. I was a
moth or flame? I'm all at sea. It all be -

Eb Bb7 Cm Bb7 Eb Bb7 Eb Bb7 Eb Bb7 F7
fool to fall And get that way; Heigh-ho! A - las! and al -
gan so well, But what an end! This is the time a fel -
Bb7 Eb9 Ab+5 Eb9 Eb+5 Ab
- so, Lack - a - day! Al - though I can't dis - miss
- ler needs a friend, When ev - 'ry hap - py plot
Eb6
Fm7 Cm Fm7 F#dim Eb G9 Cm C7+5 Fm9
The mem - 'ry of his kiss, I guess he's not
Ends with the mar - riage knot, And there's no knot
dim.
Bb7 1. Eb Eb6 Eb9 Abm6 Fm A7 Bb 2. Eb Bb7 Eb Ddim Eb
for me. He's knock-ing
for me.
3
3

BLAH-BLAH-BLAH

Lyrics by IRA GERSHWIN

Music by GEORGE GERSHWIN

Gm
G7
(D♭ bass)
D♭7
C7
F6
F
learned it from the screen. (I hope you like it.)
I
mf
E♭
F
E♭
F
stud-ied all the rhymes that all the lov-ers sing;
Then
E♭
F
Fmaj7
F7
B♭
just for you I wrote this lit-tle thing.
Refrain:
B♭
G
Bdim
F7
Blah, Blah, Blah, blah moon,
Blah, Blah, Blah a-bove,
p-mf

B♭
Gm B♭7 A7
Blah, Blah, Blah, blah croon, Blah, Blah, Blah, blah love.
Dm G7 C Am7
Tra la la la, tra la la la la, mer - ry month of
mp
C Cm F7 B♭ Bdim
May; Tra la la la, tra la la la la, 'neath the clouds of
Cm7 Dm D♭m F7 B♭ G Bdim F7
gray. Blah, Blah, Blah your hair, Blah, Blah, Blah your
p

Bb
Bb7
Eb
eyes; Blah, Blah, Blah, blah care, Blah, Blah, Blah, blah
mf
Ebm
Bb
Dm
Bb
Cm
Gm
A7
skies. Tra la la la, tra la la la la,
D7+5
G9
C7
Bb
Gm7
Cm9
F7
cot - tage for two, Blah, Blah, Blah, blah, blah dar-ling with
p
1.
Bb
F#7
Bb6
B9
C9
G7+5
C9
F7+5
you.
2.
Bb
F#7
Bb6
B9
Bb6
you.
mf
mf

DELISHIOUS

Lyrics by IRA GERSHWIN

Music by GEORGE GERSHWIN

Bbm9 Eb7 Ab6 Fm9 Fm7-5 Eb Bbm C7+5
phase of you Just seems to baf-fle my de-scrip-tive powers Four and twen-ty hours of ev - 'ry
Fm Bb7 Fm Bb7 Bbm7 Eb7
day. What can I say? What is the thing I'd love to
Ab Fm7 Ebmaj7 Cm6 Bb9
sing? I've said you're mar-vel -ous; I've said you're won-der - ful; And yet that's
Eb6 Edim Fm7 Edim Fm7 Bb11 Bb7
not it, Now let me see, I think I've got it!

Refrain: (gracefully)
Bb7 Cm6 Bm6
Eb
Bb+5
Eb6
You're so De - lish - i - ous
And so cap -
a tempo
p - mf
Bb7
Fm C-5 C7+5 C7 Fm7
rish - i - ous;
I grow am - bish - i - ous To
3
Bb7
Eb
Cm6 Bm6
have you care for me.
In that con -
Eb
Bb+5
Eb6
Bb7
nec - shi - on
You're my se - lec - shi - on

Fm C-5 C7+5 C7
Fm7
Bb7
For true af - fec - shi - on For all the time to
Eb
D7
be. Oh, I've had one, two, three, four, five, Six, sev-en, eight,
mf
Gm D7 Gm
D7
nine, ten girls be - fore; But now there's one, and you're the one, The
G Eb Cm6 Bm6
Eb
Bb+5
one girl I a - dore, 'Cause you're De - lish - i - ous,
p
a tempo

Eb6
Bb7
Fm C-5 C C7+5 C7
And so cap - rish - i - ous,
If I'm re - pe -
Fm7
Bb7
Fm Abm
1.
Eb
Cm7 Fm7
tish - i - ous, It's 'cause you're so De - lish - i - ous!
mf
3
Bb9
Cm6 Bm6
2.
Eb
Fm7 Abmaj7 Eb6
You're so De - lish - i - ous!
f

WINTERGREEN FOR PRESIDENT

Lyrics by IRA GERSHWIN

Music by GEORGE GERSHWIN

to Coda
Win-ter-green For Pres-i - dent!
He's the man the
mp
mf
mp
peo-ple choose;
Loves the I-rish and the Jews,
f
p
Ta ta ta ta ta ta ta!
f
Win - ter-green For Pres-i - dent!
Win-ter-green For
R.H.
mp
mf
mp

Pres-i-dent!
Ta ta ta ta ta
ta!
Ta ta ta ta, Win-ter-green For
Pres-i - dent!
Ta ta ta
ta ta ta!
Win - ter-green For
mf
f
ff
mf
f
ff
mp

Pres - i - dent!
Ah
Ah
He's the man the peo - ple choose;
Loves the I - rish and the Jews! Ta ta
ta, ta ta ta ta ta ta ta, ta ta ta ta ta ta, ta ta
mf
p
f
ff

D.S.
ta ta ta ta ta!
D.S.
CODA
All: Win-ter-green For Pres-i-dent! Win-ter-green For Pres-i-dent!
R.H.
dim.
Win-ter-green For Pres-i-dent! Win-ter-green For Pres-i-dent!
poco a poco cresc.
Ah!
sf

OF THEE I SING

Lyrics by IRA GERSHWIN

Music by GEORGE GERSHWIN

G Am7 Gmaj7 Am7 G D7sus4
You're the dream girl of the sweet - est sto - ry ev - er
mp
G D7sus4 D7 Gmaj9
told, A dream I've sought, Both night and day For years through
C7sus4 C7 Fmaj9 F#m7 B7 B9 B7-9
all the U. S. A. The star I've hitched my wag - on
Em Am9 D7sus4 D7 G9 G7
to Is ver - y ob - vi - ous - ly you.
poco rit.

Slowly (with expression)
Refrain:
C
C7+5
F
Dm
G7
Of Thee I Sing, ba - by,
p
C
Cmaj7
C7
F6
Dm7-5
Sum - mer, Au - tumn, Win - ter, Spring, ba - by,
C
E9
E+5
Am
Am7
D7
G
D
You're my sil - ver lin - ing, You're my sky of blue;
Em
Cm6
G
D7
G
B♭m6
D7
G7
There's a love light shin - ing, Just be - cause of you.
mf

C C7+5 F Dm G7 C
Of Thee I Sing, ba - by, You have got that
mp
C7+5 F6 E7 Am E7 Am Edim Dm Edim Dm
cer-tain thing, ba - by! Shin - ing star and in - spi - ra - tion
poco a poco cresc.
Am E7 Am Edim Dm Edim Dm Cdim C Am7 Dm7 G7
Worth - y of a might - y na - tion Of Thee I
mf
piu f ed espr.
pesante
1. C Cmaj7 C7 F G7
Sing.
2. C Fm7 C
Sing.
f
f

LOVE IS SWEEPING THE COUNTRY

Lyrics by IRA GERSHWIN

Music by GEORGE GERSHWIN

Gdim
Bb7
Gdim
Bb7
Cdim
Rich man, poor man, thief,
Doc - tor, law - yer, chief,
Feel a feel - ing
Eb
Cb9
Fb
that they can't ig - nore,
It plays a part
In ev - 'ry
mf
F7
Bb11
Bb6
Bb11
heart,
And ev - 'ry heart is shout - ing "En - core!"
Refrain:
Eb6
Bbdim
Love Is Sweep - ing The Coun - try,
Waves are hug -
sfz
f
sfz

Bb9 Edim Bb9 Bb7 Ab7 A7 Bb7 Bbdim Cdim Ddim Bbdim
- ging the shore, All the sex - es From
Cm6 Ddim Bbdim Cm6 F7-5 Eb Cdim Fm7
Maine to Tex - as Have nev - er known such love be - fore.
Bb9 Eb6 Eb9 Bbm7 Eb7
See them bill - ing and coo - ing,
sfz
Ab6 Gb7-5 F13 Abm6 Eb6
Like the bird - ies a - bove, Each girl and boy
sfz

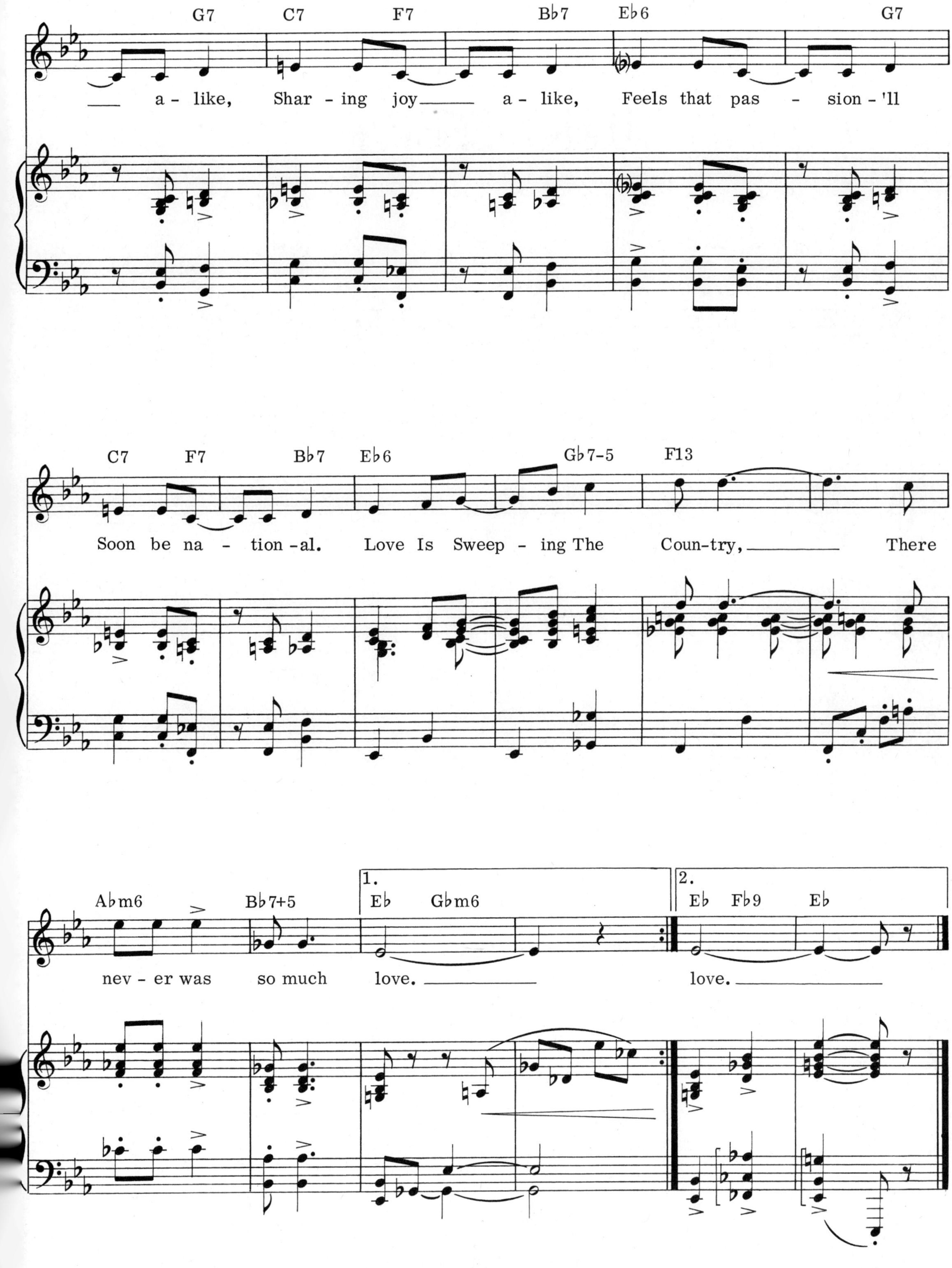

G7 C7 F7 B♭7 E♭6 G7

a - like, Shar - ing joy a - like, Feels that pas - sion - 'll

WHO CARES?

Lyrics by IRA GERSHWIN

Music by GEORGE GERSHWIN

Em Am Em7 Am6 Gmaj7
I love you and you love me And that's how it will al-ways be, And noth- ing else can
Am7 D7 Dm7 G7 C A♭9 D7-5
ev - er mean a thing.
Who Cares what the pub - lic
G B♭m Cm6 G7 G A♭9 D7-5 G G7 Em
chat - ters?
Love's the on- ly thing that mat - ters.
rit.
Refrain: (in a lilting manner)
G7 Cmaj7 B7+5 E7+5 E7 A7+5 A7 Dm7-5
Who Cares if the sky cares to fall in the sea?
mp - mf

C Dm C Cdim Dm7 Em G7 C G7 Am7
Who Cares how his - to - ry rates me? Long as your
Ab9 D7+(-9) G7 Cmaj7 B7+5 E7+5 E7
kiss in - tox - i - cates me! Why should I care? Life is
Am D9 D7-5 Ab7 C Cdim Dm7 G6
one long ju - bi - lee, So long as I care for you
G7 A7+5 Dm7 G7
And you care for me.
1. C A9-5 Ab9 G11 G7
me. Who
2. C Ab9 G9 C
me.
f

WHO CARES?
(So Long As You Care For Me)

SAM HARRIS PRESENTS
OF THEE I SING
A MUSICAL COMEDY
BOOK BY GEORGE KAUFMAN AND MORRIE RYSKIND
DIRECTED BY GEORGE KAUFMAN
LYRICS BY IRA GERSHWIN
MUSIC BY GEORGE GERSHWIN
NEW WORLD MUSIC
HARMS

George, DuBose Heyward and Ira, creators of Porgy and Bess *(1935)*.

George in a splendid setting in Hollywood (1931).

In Newark, N.J., about to leave for Hollywood for a second time (1936).

FASCINATING RHYTHM

Hands across the net: Harold Arlen and Ira in Beverly Hills. A photo snapped by George (1937).

SECOND RHAPSODY

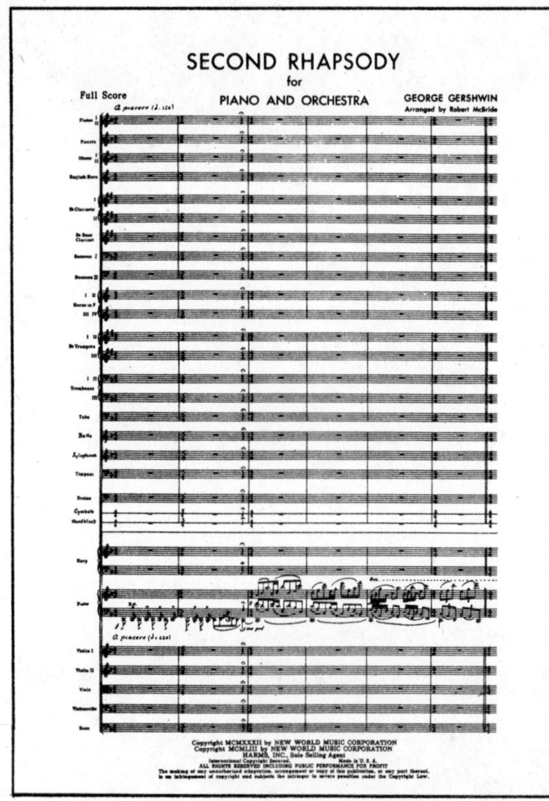

This return to the piano-with-orchestra writing for Gershwin grew out of a trip to California in 1930-31, when the brothers went to Hollywood to write their first film songs for *Delicious.* The score called for a mere handful of songs (most of them reworked Gershwin items that had not been used before for some reason or other) and an extended orchestral sequence which, in the script, was called "Manhattan Rhapsody." In this portion of the film the heroine (winsomly portrayed by Janet Gaynor), a bewildered immigrant, is shown wandering, with proper awe, through the skyscrapered streets of New York.

Producing the songs did not take long, which left time for Ira Gershwin to read or golf—or to listen to his brother's evolving rhapsody.

Because he had selected a rather sinister reiterative piano theme to open the piece, Gershwin for a time thought of calling it "Rhapsody in Rivets." This coincided with the script's shots of tall buildings beautifully. But Gershwin had a larger work in mind than the script called for; what was heard in the film was a capsule version of the longer work he had projected.

When they returned to Manhattan in February of 1931, the Gershwins not only brought back some preliminary work on what would become the Pulitzer Prize winning *Of Thee I Sing* but also the draft of what George eventually decided to name simply his *Second Rhapsody.* Near the end of May he put the final touches to the orchestration and pronounced the work finished.

"In many respects," he wrote a friend, "such as orchestration and form, it is the best thing I've written." He was striving for an entirely different musical effect as compared with his earlier rhapsody and the concerto. As he pointed out, "although the piano has quite a few solo parts, I may just make it one of the orchestral instruments instead of solo."

Curiously, unlike any other large Gershwin composition, the *Second Rhapsody* was not hurried into a performance practically before the ink was dry. For a time it seemed that Toscanini was interested in the premiere—although he had never attempted a performance of a Gershwin work up to that time. (When he did, after the composer's death, the results were not very successful).

The first performance, then, of the *Second Rhapsody* did not occur until January 29, 1932 with the Boston Symphony under Koussevitzky with the composer as pianist. It did not become an instant hit as had the earlier concert works; undoubtedly this is because it is a much less romantic, more austere work. What was overlooked, however—at least by those seeking a revival of the spirit of the first rhapsody—was that during the seven years between them Gershwin had matured musically. His orchestral skill had developed and he had other things to say tonally—his blues had taken on a darker hue. The *Second Rhapsody* remains one of his most enigmatic, most fascinating compositions, presaging the Gershwin to come. Tragically, he was denied the time.

In Hollywood, 1931, in the house in which Garbo had once lived and where the Gershwins wrote their first film score for Delicious *and George began the* Second Rhapsody.

Creators of the Pulitzer Prize-winning Of Thee I Sing; *with Ira and George, George S. Kaufman, left, and Morrie Ryskind, the librettists.*

CUBAN OVERTURE

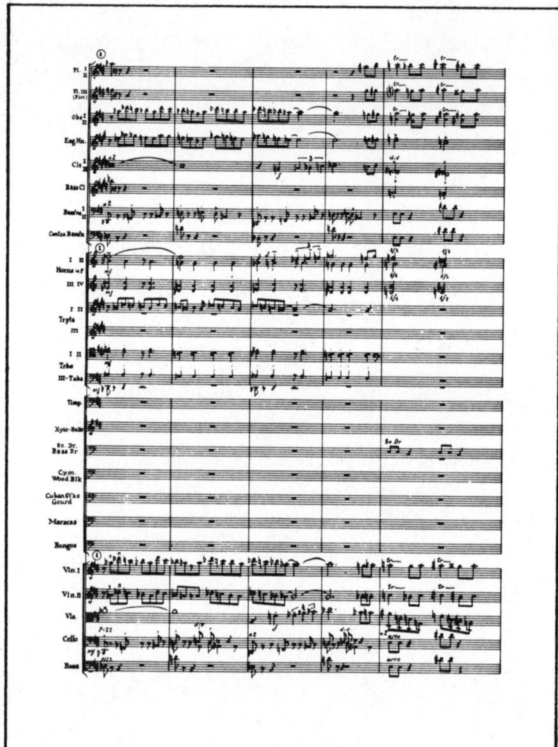

Originally entitled "Rumba," the *Cuban Overture* was a musical souvenir of a short trip to Havana in the spring of 1932. When he returned to New York, Gershwin not only had the conception of a new composition in mind but also had a set of the instruments he wished to feature in it: Cuban sticks, bongos, maracas and a gourd.

In July he set to work on the composition, began orchestration on August first and was ready for its first performance at a Lewisohn Stadium All-Gershwin Concert on August 16, 1932 in New York City. Although a musically straightforward work (it is primarily a study in rhythms and counterpoint), the *Cuban Overture* is an extraordinarily complex one—particularly because of those rhythms and in the balancing of the forces of the orchestra. In it the composer drew upon his lessons with the theorist, Joseph Schillinger (it is interesting to note that, despite his success, he always remained an insatiable student of the technicalities of his art). In his own analysis of the piece he refers to "a gradually developing canon in a polytonal manner" and to a "climax based on an ostinato of the theme of the canon." This was obviously not the Gershwin who had practically tossed off *Rhapsody in Blue,* nor the one who—with a gleam in his eye—described the first movement of the *Concerto in F* as being in "sonata form . . . but." This was the Gershwin who was on the threshold of the creation of another American masterpiece, *Porgy and Bess.*

While the *Cuban Overture* is a delightful travel piece (although a sensitive one, for it can be poorly performed), Gershwin's handling of the orchestra and complex thematic ideas points toward the fruition that would come with his folk opera.

LORELEI

Lyrics by IRA GERSHWIN

Music by GEORGE GERSHWIN

F
Fmaj7
G9-5
C7+5
C7
F
Fmaj7
Em7-5
A7
She had a yen for all the sail-ors, Fish-er-men and gobs and whal-ers;
Dm7
G7
C
Dm7
G7
C
She had a most im-mor-al eye, They called her Lor-e-lei;
Gm
Gm7
C9
Fmaj7
F7
Gm7
C7
F
F7
Dm
F7
She cre-a-ted quite a stir And I want to be like her.
mf
Refrain:
B♭
E♭maj7
B♭maj7
B♭6
E♭
I want to be like that gal on the riv-er, Who sang her
p-mf

Bb Bb7 Ebmaj7 Eb6 Cm7-5 Bb Cm Dm Eb
song to the ships pass-ing by; She had the goods and how she could de -
cresc.
Am G+5 C9 C7 F Cm F C7+5 F9 Eb
liv - er The Lor - e - lei! She used to
Bb Ebmaj7 Bbmaj7 Bb6 Eb Bb Bb7
love in a strange kind of fash-ion, With lots of hey! ho - de - ho! hi - de-
Ebmaj7 Eb6 Cm7-5 Bb Cm Dm Bb7
hi! And I can guar - an - tee I'm full of

C9 C9-5 F7 B♭ Cm7 B♭ Em7-5 A7-9
pas-sion Like the Lor - e - lie. I'm
mp
Dm Gm6 B♭ A7
treach-er-ous Ja! Ja! Oh, I just can't hold my-
Dm A7 A7-9 D Em7 E7
self in check. I'm lech-er-ous Ja! Ja! I want to
A G F♯m Em D Edim F7 F9 B♭ E♭maj7
bite my in-i-tials on a sail-or's neck! Each af-fair has a kick and a
mp

B♭maj7 B♭6 E♭ B♭ B♭7 E♭maj7 E♭6 Cm7-5
wal- lop, For what they crave I can al - ways sup - ply, I
B♭ Cm Dm B♭7 C9 C9-5 F7
1.
B♭ E♭ B♭ C7-5 F7 E♭
want to be just like that oth -er trol-lop The Lor - e-lei! I want to
2.
B♭ E♭ B♭ C7 G♭7 F7+5 B♭
Lor - e - lei!
mf
sf

ISN'T IT A PITY?

Lyrics by IRA GERSHWIN

Music by GEORGE GERSHWIN

F6 G7 C B7 E7-5 A7
rhyme? Is-n't It A Pit-y? Is-n't it a crime?
rive, All my Dres-den boy friends were on-ly half a-live.
cresc.
D9 Fm6
My jour-ney's end-ed; Ev-'ry-thing is splen-did;
Sleep-y was Her-mann, Fritz was like a ser-mon,
C Am6 B7 Em Cmaj7
Meet-ing you to-day Has giv-en me a
Hans was such a bore! How well you planned it!
Em7 A9 D7sus4 D7 G11 G6 G G7+5
won-der-ful i-dea, Here I stay!
I just could-n't stand it An-y more!

Refrain: not fast, with expression
C Em7 F G9+5 Em A7
It's a fun-ny thing, I look at you_ I get a thrill_
p-mf con calore
Dm7 G9 C C7 F Em Dm7 G11
I nev-er knew,_ Isn't It A Pit-y we nev-er met_ be-
C Adim F C Gm6 G7+5 C Em7
fore? Here we are at last!
F G9+5 Em A7 Dm7 G9
It's like a dream!_ The two of us_ A per-fect team!_

C C7 F Em Dm7 G11 C Cmaj7 Dm7 G7
Is - n't It A Pit - y we nev-er met_ be - fore?
C Am6 Em F♯m7 B7
Im - ag - ine all the lone - ly years we've wast - ed:
Im - ag - ine all the lone - ly years you've wast - ed:
mf
Em A7 G6 G
You, with the neigh-bors, I, at sil - ly la - bors; What joys un -
Fish - ing for sal - mon, Los-ing at back-gam-mon. What joys un -
Am7 D7 G11 F9
tast - ed! You, read - ing Hei-ne, I, some-where in Chin-a.
tast - ed! My nights were sour,_ Spent with Scho-pen-hau-er.

C Em7 F G9+5
Hap - pi - est of men I'm sure to be,
Let's for - get the past, Let's both a - gree
Em A7 Dm7 G9
If on - ly you will say to me,
That I'm for you And you're for me,
C C9 C9+5 Fmaj7 Em7 Dm7 G9
ten.
"It's an aw - ful pit - y, We nev - er, nev - er met be -
And it's such a pit - y, We nev - er, nev - er met be -
1. C Cmaj7 C6 C Dm7 G9 G7+5
2. C F♯7 G7 C
fore."
fore."
p
mf
sf

MY COUSIN IN MILWAUKEE

Lyrics by IRA GERSHWIN

Music by GEORGE GERSHWIN

E♭
Am7-5
D7
Gm
Em7-5
A7+5
sang in a low - down way.
She was a pos - i -tive sen-
mf
D7sus4
D7
Gm
Em7-5
A7+5
sa - tion;
The songs that she sang would nev - er
R.H.
D7sus4
D7
G
C9
B9
B♭9
A9
miss.
My cous - in was my in - spir -
R.H.
D7+5
D7
G7
Em7-5
F9(6)
F9+5
a - tion,
That's how I got like this!

Refrain:
Tacet
Ab Gm Fm Gm Ab Gm Fm Gm
I got a cous - in in Mil- wau - kee;
She's got a
p-f poco pesante
Ab Gm Fm Gm Ab Gm Fm Ab
voice so squaw- ky,
And though she's
Db Cm Bbm Cm
tall and kind of gaw - ky,
mf
Db Cm Bbm Ab9 Bb+5 Eb6 Cm7 F7sus4
Oh, how she gets the men!
Her sing-ing
Ab Gm Fm Gm Ab Gm Fm Gm
is - n't op - er - at - ic,
It's got a
p

Ab Gm Fm Gm Ab Gm Fm Ab Db Cm Bbm Cm
lot of sta - tic, But makes your heart get ac - ro-bat - ic
Db Cm Bbm Ab9 Bb+5 Eb6 G7
Nine times out of ten. When
mf
Cm Cm(Bbbass) Am7-5 Ab7 G7 Cm Cm6
she sings hot you can't be sol-emn, It sends the shiv - ers up and down your
Dm7 G7 Cm Cm(Bbbass) Am7-5 Ab7 G7
spin - al col-umn; When she sings blue, the men shout, "What stuff!

C9 F9(6) Ab Gm Fm Gm
That ba-by is hot stuff!" So if you like the way I sing songs,
Ab Gm Fm Gm Ab Gm Fm Gm Ab Gm Fm G7
If you think that I'm a wow, You can
Cm Abm6 Eb Ab Eb F9 Bb7 F7-5 Eb7-5 Ab7 Bb11
thank my squaw-ky cous-in from Mil-wau-kee, be-cause she taught me
cresc.
Eb Cm7 F13 F7sus4 Eb D Eb D Eb Fb Eb
how! how!
più f

MINE

Lyrics by IRA GERSHWIN

Music by GEORGE GERSHWIN

G7 C7+ F6 D7+ G7 C7+ F6 Fmaj7 Dm Fmaj7
3
you are mine, Nev-er an - oth - er Val - en -
3

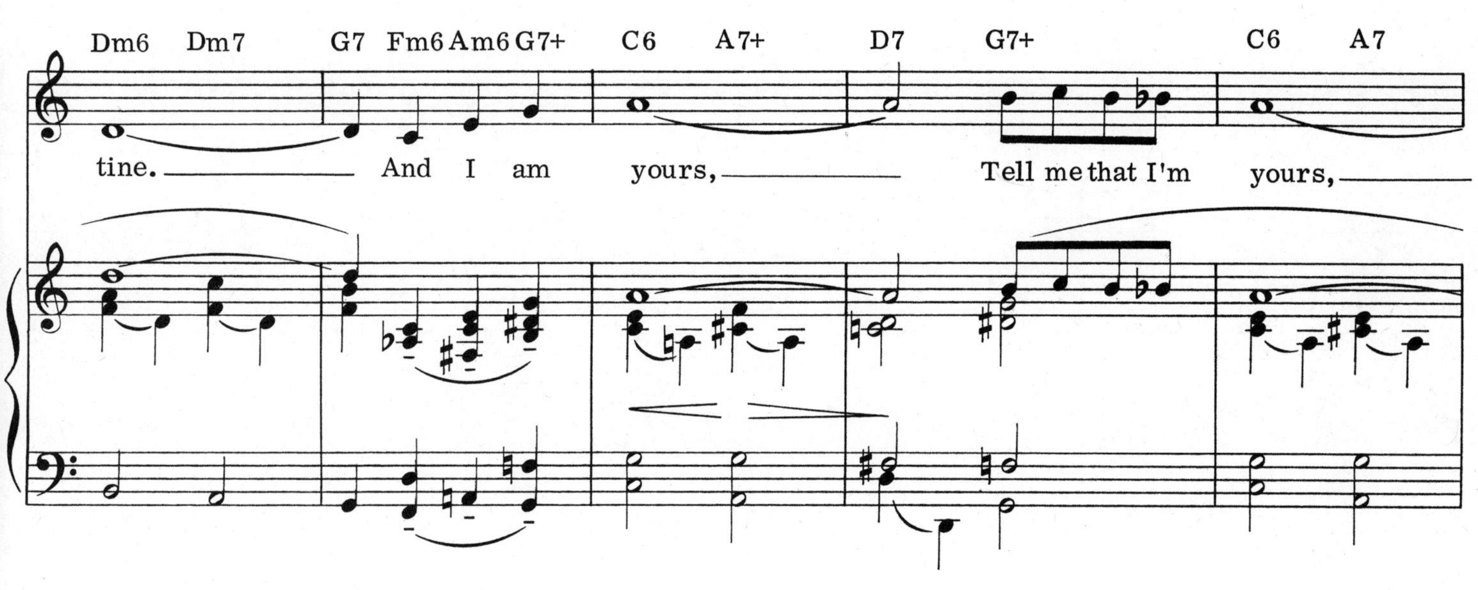
Dm6 Dm7 G7 Fm6 Am6 G7+ C6 A7+ D7 G7+ C6 A7
tine. And I am yours, Tell me that I'm yours,

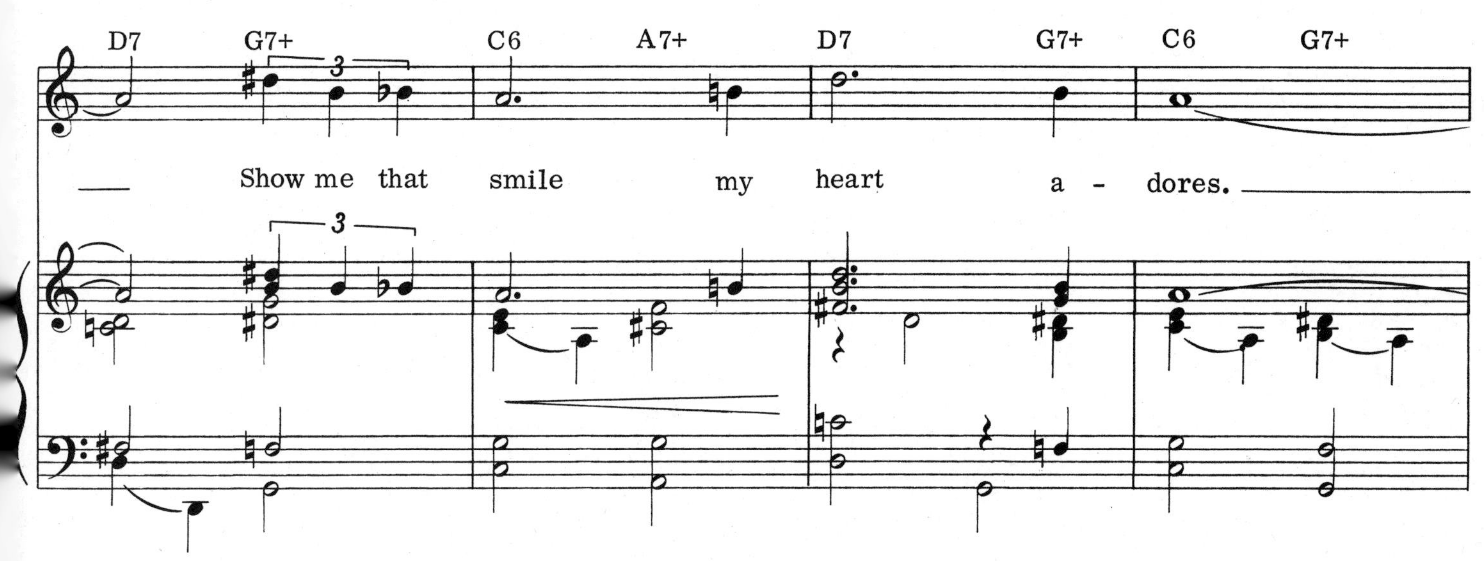
D7 G7+ C6 A7+ D7 G7+ C6 G7+
3
Show me that smile my heart a - dores.
3

C9 C7-9 C7 F E7 E♭maj7 D9 Cmaj7 B7 E7 A7
Mine, more than di - vine To
Dm7 G11 C D9 Cm6 D9-5 G7+
know that love like yours is mine.
(1st Time Top line only, 2nd Time both)
C6 A7+ D7 G7+ C6 A7+
The point they're mak- ing in the song Is that they more than
Mine, love is mine,
mp - mf

D7 G7+ C6 A7+ D7 G7+
get a - long And he is not a - shamed to say
Wheth - er it's rain or storm or
C6 G7+ C9 F#m6 C7 F6 D7+
She made him what he is to - day. It does a per - son
shine. Mine,
G7 C7+ F6 D7+ G7 C7+
good to see Such hap - py do - mes - ti - ci - ty,
you are mine, Nev - er an -

F6
Am
Dm7
G7
Dm7
G7
Fm6 Am6 G7+
The way they're mak-ing love, you'd swear
They're not a mar-ried pair,
oth - er Val - en - tine.
And I am
C6
A7+
D7
G7+
C6
A7+
He says no mat - ter what oc - curs,
What - ev - er he may
yours,
Tell me that I'm yours,
D7
G7+
C6
A7+
D7
G7+
have is hers,
The point that she is mak - ing is,
Show me that smile my heart a -

C6 G7+ C9 F♯m6 C7 F E7 E♭maj7 D9
3
What-ev-er she may have is his, Mine, more than di-
dores. Mine, more than di-
3
3
Cmaj7 B7 E7 A7 Dm7 G11
vine To know that love like yours is
vine To know that love like yours is
1. C D9 Cm6 D9-5 G7+
2. C C6
Mine.
Mine.
Mine.
Mine.

LET 'EM EAT CAKE

Lyrics by IRA GERSHWIN

Music by GEORGE GERSHWIN

A Gm A Gm A Gm A Eb7 Em7 A7
break! From now on you'll be eat - ing
Dm Bb7 Dm Gm9 C7 Fmaj7 F6
cake! Ensemble: We've al-ways want- ed cake, At
mp
Gm9 C7 A7 D Fm D Fm D Am D Fm
last we get that break. Wintergreen: With drums a - boom - ing and our flag un -
mf
A Gm A Gm A Gm A Eb7 A9
furled, This is what I'm tell - ing the

D
D+5
D
G
world:
Ensemble: Com-rades, it is clear The mil-
mf
len - i - um is here!
D7-5
G7
L.H.
ff
Tempo di Marcia (with spirit)
C
Am
C
Am Bm
Am Bm D7
Wint: Let 'Em Eat Cake! The land of free-dom is free once
deciso
mf - f
6/8 = ¢
G11
G7
G11
G7
F
Em
C
Dm
Em Dm
more.
p

C Am C Am Bm Am B7
Let 'Em Eat Cake! Let there be sun-shine from shore to
f
6/8 = ¢
E11 E7 E11 E7 D C♯m A Bm C♯m Bm
shore.
mf
R.H.
2
Am7 A9 D7 G Gmaj7 G♯dim
Now is the time to be wak - ing! Come on, let's start!
mp
Am7 Am9 D7 G9 F G Am G7 C G9
Now is the time to be tak - ing your part!

C Am C Am Bm Am B7 Am
Let 'Em Eat Cake! Good times are com -ing the skies are
mf
6/8 = ¢
C C6 Cmaj7 C6 Em C A7
clear!
f
Dm G11 G7-9 C A7 Dm
Let it be known the whole world o - ver, The new
mf
più f
G11 G7 1. C Cdim G11 2. C
day is here! here!
f marcato
f marcato
sf
sf

Curtain call, opening night of *Porgy and Bess* in Boston (1935).

George visiting the set of *Shall We Dance* (1936).

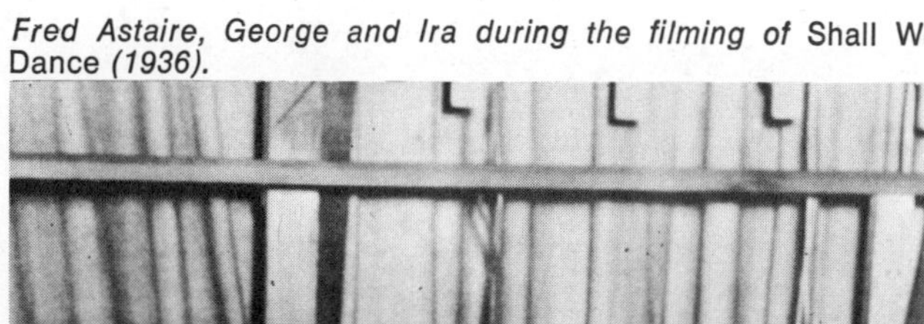

Fred Astaire, George and Ira during the filming of *Shall We Dance* (1936).

At the keyboard (1934).

Café Sacher, Vienna: Ira and Leonore Gershwin, George and, to his left, composer Emmerich Kalman (1928).

BLUE BLUE BLUE

Lyrics by IRA GERSHWIN

Music by GEORGE GERSHWIN

that's why we're paint-ing the White House blue!
rit.
Refrain: Moderato (slowly, with expression)
C Am7 D7 G7 G7+5 C F♯dim
Blue, Blue, Blue! Not pink or pur-ple or yel-low, Not
p-f
G7 G7+5 C E7 Am Am7
brown like Mis-ter O-thel-lo, But Blue, Blue,
D9 G7 Edim F7 E7
Blue! The coun-try clam-ored for some-bod-y new, And grew e-
mf

C♯dim D7 D7-5 G7 C Am7 D7
nam-ored of Win-ter-green who gave us Blue, Blue, Blue, The
G7 G7+5 C F♯dim G7 G7+5
col - or Heav-en is paint - ed; What col - or could be more
C E7 Am Am7 D9 C
saint-ed Than Blue, Blue, Blue? The U. S. A. is a
C7 A7 Dm7 G7 1. C F G7 2. C F C
Blue S. A., It's a dream come true. true.
mf
f

SUMMERTIME

Lyrics by DuBOSE HEYWARD

Music by GEORGE GERSHWIN

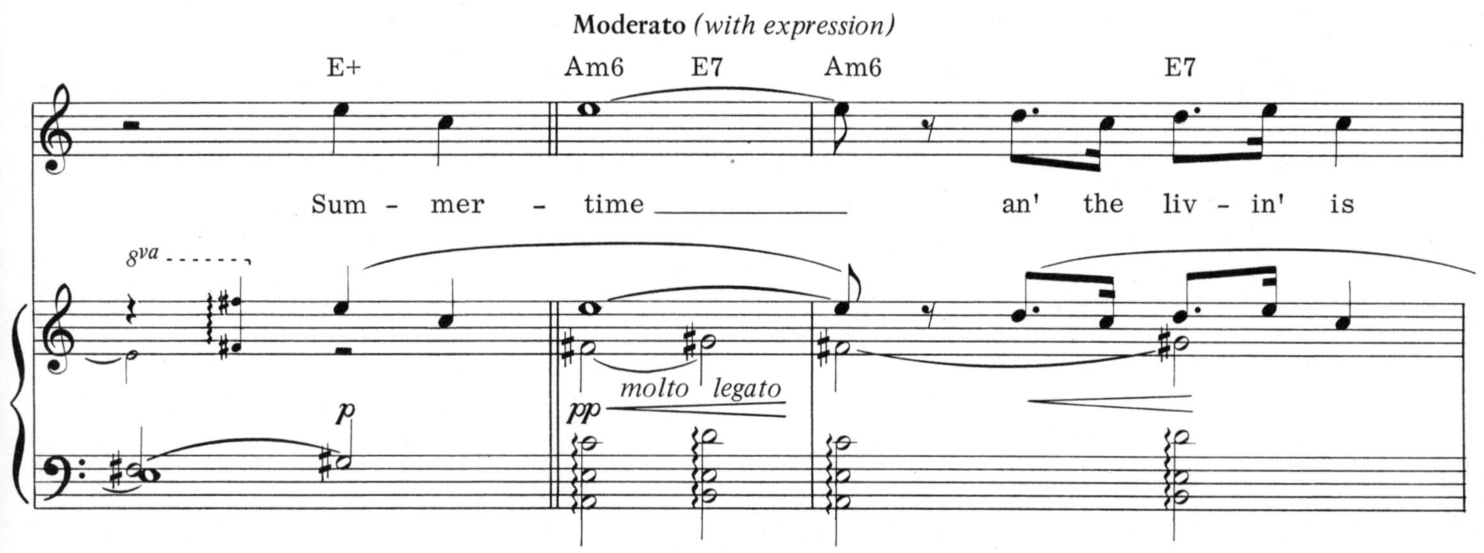

Am6 E7 Am6 E7 Am6 Dm F
eas - y, Fish are jump - in',
Fmaj7 D♯dim E B7 E Em6 E7-5
an' the cot - ton is high. Oh yo'
poco rit.
mf a tempo
Am6 E7 Am6 E7 Am6 E7
dad - dy's rich, an' yo' ma is good - look - in',
Am D7 C Am D G11
So hush, lit - tle ba - by, don' yo'

Am
E+5
Am6
E+5
cry.
8va
poco animato
D9
E+5
3
Am6
E7
Am6
E7
One of these morn - in's
You goin' to rise up
8va
3
poco rit.
a tempo
Am6
E7
Am6
E7
Am6
Dm
F
sing - in',
Then you'll spread yo' wings
3
3
Fmaj7
D♯dim
E
B7
E
Em6
E7-5
an' you'll take the sky.
But till that

Am6
E7
Am6
E7
Am6
E7
morn - in'
there's a noth - in' can harm you
Am
D7
C
Am
D
G11
With Dad - dy an' Mam - my stand - in'
3
Am
D
G11
C
F9
B♭
E7(6)
by.
mp
dim.
Am
Am6
8va
ten.
morendo
pp

MY MAN'S GONE NOW

Lyrics by DuBOSE HEYWARD

Music by GEORGE GERSHWIN

(wailing)
mp
Ah,
Ah,
rall.
a tempo
Ole Man Sor - row's come to keep me
a tempo
rall.
com - p'ny, Whis-per-in' be - side me when I say my prayers.
p
Ah,

Animato
mp
Ah,
Ain' dat I min'
poco accel.
f
rit.
mp
work-in'
Work an' me is trav - el - ers Jour - ney-in' to -
3
sub. rall.
mf
ged - der to de prom - ise land.
But
f
sub. rall.
(increasing in voice)
a tempo e poco cresc.
Ole Man Sor - row's march-in' all de way wid me,
mf a tempo e poco cresc.
3

Meno
f
Tell - in' me I'm ole now Since I lose my man.
f pesante
mf espr.
Chorus: Since she lose her man.
p
Serena: Since I lose my man.
mf espr.
p
a tempo
Chorus: Ah,
Ah,
mf
Serena: Ole Man
a tempo
mp
Sor - row sit - tin' by de fire - place, Ly - in' all night

poco rall.
Più mosso
p
long by me in de bed. Tell - in' me de
poco rall.
p
same thing morn - in', noon an' eb' - nin', That I'm all a -
Meno
lone now Since my man is dead.
p
mf (wailing) gliss.
f
ff sub. allarg.
Ah, Since my man
p cresc.
R.H.
mf
ff sub. allarg.

Grandioso
a tempo
(all sway to rhythm)
is
dead.
ff a tempo
Serena & Chorus: (wailing)
p gliss.
(approximate notes)
poco cresc.
mf rit.
mp meno
poco cresc.
mf rit.
freely
rit.
Serena:
Ah!
fp
rit.
col.8va

I GOT PLENTY O' NUTTIN'

Lyrics by IRA GERSHWIN & DuBOSE HEYWARD | Music by GEORGE GERSHWIN

E A E C♯ D G Am7
got no mis - er - y. De folks wid plen - ty o'
Gmaj7 Am7 G Am7 G B7 E A
plen-ty Got a lock on de door, 'Fraid some-bod-y's a -
E A E A E C♯ D
go - in' to rob 'em while dey's out a - mak - in' more. What
G Am7 Gmaj7 G Bm E7sus4 Bm6 Em
for? I got no lock on de door, (dat's no way to

Bm E7sus4 Bm6 Em Bm E9sus4 Bm6 Em
be.) Dey kin steal de rug from de floor, Dat's o-keh wid
Bm Am7 D Am7 D7
me, 'Cause de things dat I prize, Like de stars in de skies, all are free.
marcato e cresc.
G Am7 Gmaj7 Am7 D7
Oh, I Got Plen-ty O' Nut-tin', An'
f p
G Am7 G B7 E A E A
nut-tin's plen-ty fo' me. I got my gal, got my song, got

E A E C♯
(Spoken in high voice)
3
D
Heb-ben the whole day long.
No use com-plain-in'!
Got my
G Am7 G Dm7 G Am7 G C
gal, got my Lawd, got my
G Em7 D7(6) G Am7
song.
poch. rit.
f a tempo
R.H.
Gmaj7 Am7 G Am7 Gmaj7 Am7 D7 G Am7
I Got Plen-ty O' Nut-tin', An' nut-tin's plen-ty fo'
mp

G B7 E A E A E A E
me. I got the sun, got the moon, Got the deep blue
C# D G Am7 Gmaj7 Am7
sea. De folks wid plen - ty o' plen - ty
G Am7 G B7 E A
Got to pray all de day. Seems wid plen - ty you
E A E A E C#
sure got to wor - ry how to keep the deb - ble a - way,

D G Am7 Gmaj7 G Bm E7sus4
a - way. I ain't a fret-tin' 'bout
Bm6 Em Bm E7sus4 Bm6 Em Bm E9sus4
hell Till the time ar - rive. Nev-er wor-ry long as I'm well,
Bm6 Em Bm Am7 D Am7
Nev-er one to strive to be good, to be bad, What the hell? I is
marcato e cresc.
D7 G Am7 Gmaj7 Am7 D7
glad I's a-live. Oh, I Got Plen-ty O' Nut-tin', An'
f
p

G Am7 G B7 E A E A
nut - tin's plen - ty fo' me. I got my gal, got my song, Got
E A E C#
(Spoken in high voice)
D
Heb-ben the whole day long. No use com-plain-in'! Got my
G Am7 G Dm7 G Am7 G C
gal, got my Lawd, Got my
G C7 Gm C7-5 Bb D7 G
song.
mf cresc. ed animato
f

BESS YOU IS MY WOMAN NOW

Lyrics by DuBOSE HEYWARD
IRA GERSHWIN

Music by GEORGE GERSHWIN

D♭maj7
F9
B♭
F7
B♭
Dm
Gm7
Want no wrin - kle on yo' brow no -
A7
Em7-5
A7
D6
G7
how, be - cause de sor - row of the past is all done,
D
G♯m7-5
C♯7
F♯6
done. Oh, Bess, my Bess! De real
B7
C♯7
F♯
F♯m
A7
hap - pi - ness is jes' be - gun.
poco rit.

Tempo I° molto cantabile
D A7 A9 C A9 D F D7 Gsus4 G+5 Em7-5
Bess: Por - gy, I's yo' wom - an now, I is, I is! An'
mf più espr.
D G♯m7-5 G7 F♯m7 C7
I ain' nev-er go - in' no-where 'less you shares de fun.
stringendo
Fmaj7 A7 D A7 A9 C A9 D F♯m Bm7
Dere's no wrin - kle on my brow no -
poco rall.
a tempo
C♯7 F♯ C♯7 F♯ C♯7 D♯m A♯7
how, but I ain' go - in'! You hear me say - in', if you ain' go - in',
Subito più mosso

D♯m D7 D7-5 F♯ C♯7sus4 C♯7+5
Wid you I'm stay - in'. Por - gy, I's yo' wom - an
rall.
f a tempo
rit.
marcato
Poco sostenuto (gently)
F♯ C♯7sus4 C♯7+5 F♯6 A♯m7-5
now! I's yours for - ev - er, Morn-in' time an' ev-'nin' time an'
a tempo
rit.
p dolce
Bmaj7 G♯m F♯6 A♯m7-5
sum-mer time an' win - ter time. Porgy: Morn - in' time an' ev-'nin' time an'
pp
Bmaj7 G♯m7 F♯ F♯m6 F♯7 F♯m6 F♯ F♯dim F♯sus4 F♯
sum-mer time an' win-ter time; Bess, you got yo'
mf animando

Tempo I° molto cantabile
F♯m A7 D A7 A9 C A9
Bess:
Por - gy, I's yo' wom - an
Porgy:
man.
Bess, You Is my Wom - an
rit.
mf
D F D7 Gsus4 G+5 Em7-5 D
now, I is, I is! An' I ain' nev-er go -in' no-where
now an' for - ev - er. Dis life is jes' be - gun,
G♯m7-5 G7 F♯m7 C7 Fmaj7 A7 D
'less you shares de fun. Dere's no
Bess, we two is one now an' for - ev - er. Oh, Bess, don'
stringendo
poco rall.
mf a tempo

A7 A9 C A9 D F♯m Bm7 C♯7 F♯ C♯7
wrin - kle on my brow no - how, but I ain' go - in'!
min' dose wom - en, You got yo Por - gy, you loves yo' Por - gy, I knows you
Subito più mosso
F♯ C♯7 D♯m A♯7 D♯m D7 D7-5
You hear me say - in', if you ain' go - in', Wid you I'm stay - in'.
means it, I seen it in yo' eyes, Bess.
rall.
marcato
F♯ C♯7sus4 C♯7+5 F♯
Por - gy, I's yo' wom - an now! I's
We'll go swing - in' through de years a -
a tempo
rit.
a tempo

C♯7sus4 C♯7+5 F♯ (gently) A♯m7-5 Bmaj7 G♯m
yours for - ev - er Morn-in' time an' ev-'nin' time an' sum-mer time an' win-ter time.
(humming)
sing - in'. Hum
p
F♯ (humming) A♯m7-5 Bmaj7 G♯m7
Hum
Morn - in' time an' ev - 'nin' time an' sum - mer time an' win - ter time.
pp
F♯ F♯m6 F♯7 F♯m6 F♯ F♯dim F♯sus4 F♯ D7 F♯
Oh, my Por - gy,
My Bess,
mf
p allarg.

E♭7 C♯7 F♯ D♯m C♯7 C♯m C♯m7-5
my man Por - gy, From dis min-ute I'm tell - in' you, I keep dis vow:
my Bess, From dis min-ute I'm tell - in' you, I keep dis vow:
a tempo, dolcissimo
F♯ F♯9 F♯6 D♯m7-5 Bm7-5 F♯6 F♯9
Por - gy, I's yo' wom- an now.
Oh, my Bes - sie, we's hap - py now.
Bmaj7 G♯m C♯7(F♯bass) F♯ E F♯
We is one now!
dim.
espr. e rit.
pp

IT AIN'T NECESSARILY SO

Lyrics by IRA GERSHWIN

Music by GEORGE GERSHWIN

A7 D7 Gm C7 Eb9 D11
Ain't Ne - ces - sa - ri - ly So. Li'l
Da - vid was small, but oh
Allegro giocoso (like a savage outburst)
Gm Gm7 Eb7 Db Gbm Eb7
my! Wa - doo, All: Wa - doo,
Ab Eb7 Bdim Ab D7 Em7
Sp. L.: Zim bam bod- dle- oo, All: Zim bam boo - dle - oo, Sp.L.: Hoo - dle ah da wa da,
Fm6 D7 Gm D
All: Hoo - dle ah da wa da, Sp.L.: Scat - ty wah. All: Scat - ty wah. Sp.L.: Yeah! 3. Oh,
subito rit.

Tempo I
Gm C Gm C Gm C
Jo-nah, he lived in de whale, Oh, Jo-nah, he lived in de
Mo-ses was found in a stream, Li'l Mo-ses was found in a
mf
Gm C7 D♭7 C7 D♭7
whale, Fo' he made his home in Dat fish-s' ab-do-men. Oh,
stream, He float-ed on wa-ter Till Ole Phar-aoh's daugh-ter She
A7 D7 1. Gm C7 E♭9 D11 2. Gm Gm7
Jo-nah, he lived in de whale. Li'l
fished him, she says, from that stream.
Allegro
E♭7 D♭ G♭m E♭7 A♭ E♭7
Wa - doo, All: Wa - doo, Sp.L.: Zim bam bod-dle-oo,
mf

Bdim Ab D7 Em7 Fm6 D7
All: Zim bam bod-dle-oo, Sp.L.: Hoo-dle ah da wa da, All: Hoo-dle ah da wa da,
Gm D
Sp.L.: Scat-ty wah, All: Scat-ty wah. Sp.L.: Yeah! It
subito rit.
mp
Tempo I
Gm C Gm C Gm C Gm
Ain't Ne-ces-sa-ri-ly So, It Ain't Ne-ces-sa-ri-ly So. Dey
a tempo
C7 Db7 C7 Db7 A7 D7
tell all you chil-lun De deb-ble's a vil-lun, But 'tain't ne-ces-sa-ri-ly

Gm Eb7 Ab
so. To get in - to Heb - ben don' snap for a seb - ben! Live
mf
Am7 D7 G6 G7 C7 F
clean! Don' have no fault. Oh I takes dat gos - pel When - ev - er it's pos'-ble, But
A7(sus4) A7-5 D7+5 Gm C Gm C
wid a grain of salt. Me - thus'-lah lived nine hun-dred years. Me-
mp
Gm C Gm C7 Db7
thus - lah lived nine hun - dred years, But who calls dat liv - in' When
mf

C7 Db7 A7 D7 Gm C
no gal 'll give in To no man what's nine hun - dred years?
F#7 Eb7 Cm6 G D7
I'm preach-in' dis ser - mon to show, It
mp
un poco meno
C B7 Em Am7-5 G D9+5
ain't nes - sa, ain't nes - sa, ain't nes - sa, ain't nes - sa, ain't ne - ces - sa - ri - ly
poco a poco cresc.
rall.
G6
so.
mf a tempo
f

I LOVES YOU PORGY

Lyrics by DuBOSE HEYWARD

Music by GEORGE GERSHWIN

Animando
Some day I know he's com - in' back to call me,
p
He's goin' to han - dle me an' hol' me so.
ten.
It's goin' to be like dy - in', Por - gy, deep in - side me.
ten.
But when he calls, I know I have to go.
mf

Bess:
Porgy: Freely mf
If dere warn't no Crown, Bess, if dere was
fpp colla voce
I loves you
ten.
on - ly just you an' Por - gy, what den?
Andantino molto espressivo
Por-gy, don' let him take me, Don' let him han-dle me an' drive me

mad. If you kin keep me, I wants to stay here wid you for-
ev - er, an' I'd be glad.
poco rit.
a tempo
mf
Allegretto
f(with strength and rhythm)
Porgy: There, there, Bess, you don' need to be a -
8va
f
tr
mf marcato
fraid no mo'. You's picked up hap - pi - ness an' laid yo'
simile

wor-ries down,— You goin' to live eas - y, you goin' to live high.— You
goin' to out - shine— ev - 'ry wom- an in dis town. An' re-mem-ber,
when Crown— come that's my bus' - ness.
ff

Più appassionato, ma ben ritmato
ten. ten. ten.
Bess: I loves you, Por-gy,
Porgy: Bess,
What you think I is
Don'let him take me,
Don' let him
an-y-way, To let that dirt-y houn' dog steal my wom-an?
han-dle me
with his hot han'.
If you wants to stay wid Por-gy, you go-in' stay. You got a home now,

If you can keep me, I wants to
hon-ey, an' you got love. So no mo' cry-in', can't you un-der-stan'?
stay here wid you for - ev - er.
You go - in' to go a-bout yo' bus'-ness sing-in', 'Cause you got Por-gy,
Maestoso
I got my man.
You got a man.
rit.

BY STRAUSS

Lyrics by IRA GERSHWIN

Music by GEORGE GERSHWIN

Dm6 E7 Cm6 D7
Oh, I'd give no quar - ter to Kern or Cole Por - ter and
B♭m6 C9 F Gm
Gersh-win keeps pound-ing on tin. How can I be
mf
Fmaj7 Gm
civ - il when hear - ing this driv - el? It's on - ly for
Dm6 B♭m6 F Fmaj7 F6 E9
night club-bing sous - es. Oh, give me the free 'n' eas - y

Am7
Am6
C
D9
C
waltz that is Vi-en-nese-y And go tell the band if
G7
C
they want a hand the waltz must be Strauss's!
B♭
B♭m
C7
B♭
Ya, ya, ya! Give me
mp grazioso
Am
A♭m
C7
oom - pah - pah!
f marcato

Refrain:
Gm7
C9
F
When I want a mel - o - dy lilt -ing through the house,
mp - mf a tempo
Gm7
C7
C9+5
F6
Dm6
Then I want a mel- o - dy By Strauss! It
E7
Em7
A7
Am7
D7
Gm
Dm7
laughs! it sings! The world is in rhyme, Swing-ing to
G7
G7-5
C7
Gm7
C9
B♭m
three quar-ter time. Let the "Da-nube" flow a - long And the "Fle-der-
fp
a tempo

F Gm7 C7 C9+5 F6
maus!" Keep the wine and give me song By Strauss!
F7 Bb Db Eb F Fdim
By Jo! By Jing! "By Strauss" is the thing! So I say to
mf animato
mp calmo
3
Gm7 C9 C7+5 F F7 D7 Gm
ha-cha-cha Her - aus! Just give me a oom-pah-pah
C7 C11 1. F Db7 C7 2. F C9 F
By Strauss. When I want a Strauss.
mf
sf

LET'S CALL THE WHOLE THING OFF

Lyrics by IRA GERSHWIN

Music by GEORGE GERSHWIN

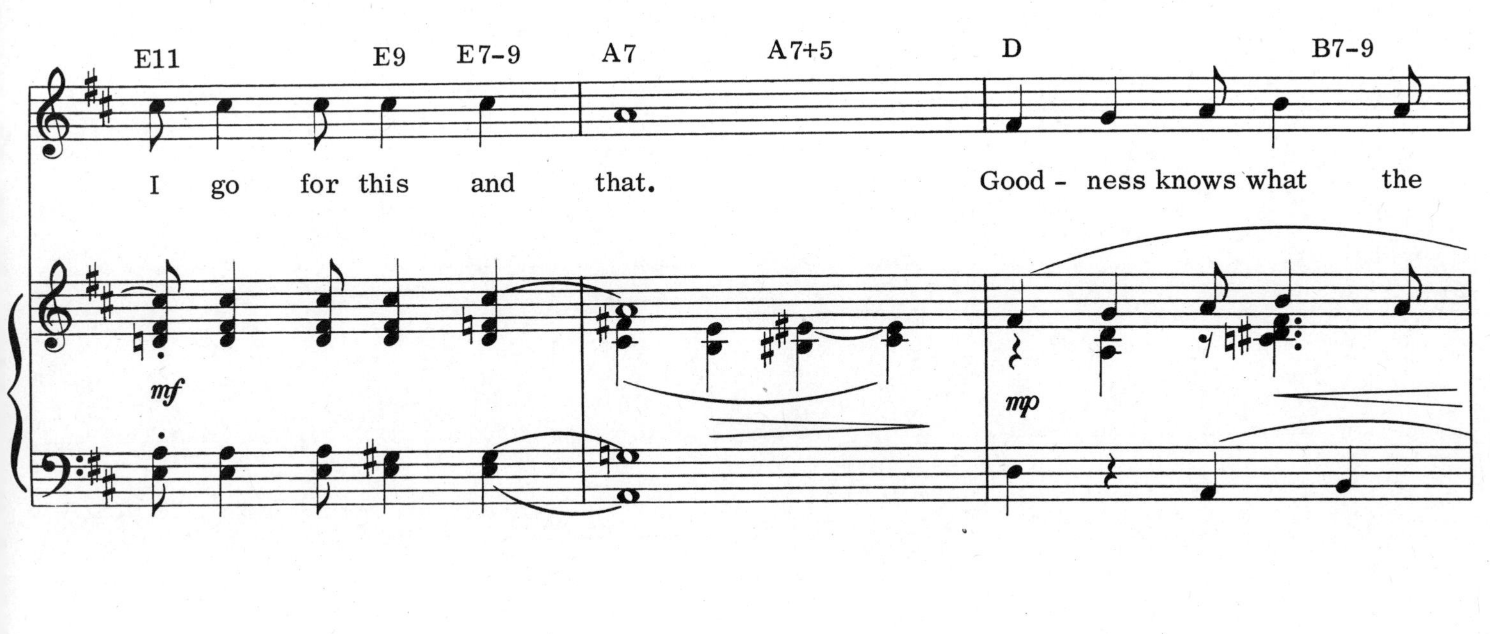
E11
E9
E7-9
A7
A7+5
D
B7-9
I go for this and that. Good - ness knows what the
mf
mp

Em
D
A7sus4
A7
D
G9
end will be; — Oh, I don't know where I'm at.... It

A6
F♯m6
E7-9
A6
looks as if we two will nev - er be one,

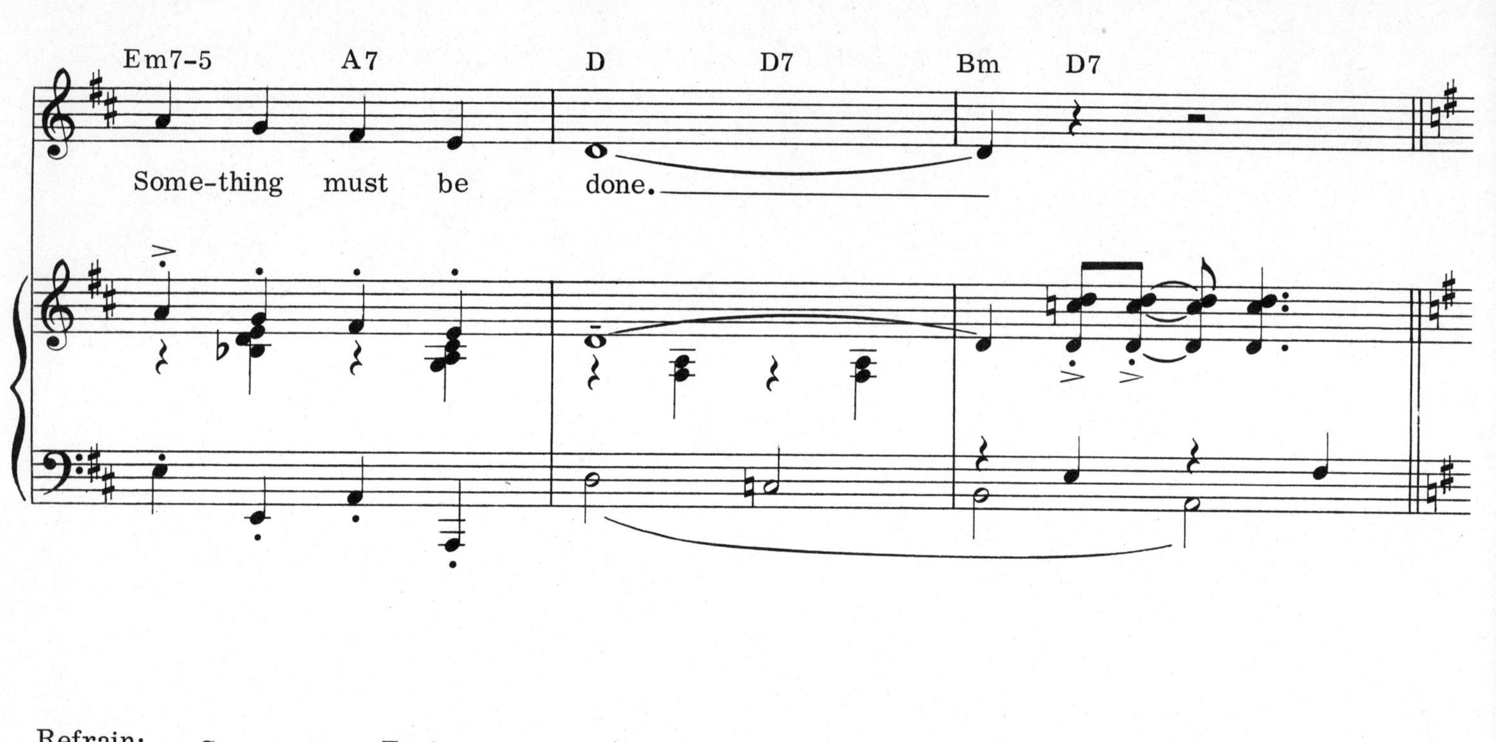
Em7-5
A7
D
D7
Bm
D7
Some-thing must be done.

Refrain:
G
Em9
Am7
D7-9
G
Em9
You say ee - ther And I say eye - ther, You say nee - ther And
You say laugh - ter And I say lawf - ter, You say af - ter And
p - mf

Am7
D7-9
G
G7
C
Cm
I say ny - ther; Ee - ther, eye - ther, nee - ther, ny - ther,
I say awf - ter; Laugh-ter, lawf - ter, af - ter, awf - ter,
mf

G Em A7 D7 G Em9
Let's Call The Whole Thing Off! You like po - ta - to and
Let's Call The Whole Thing Off! You like va - nil - la and
Am7 Cm D7 G Em9 Am7 Cm D7
I like po - tah - to, You like to - ma - to and I like to - mah - to; Po -
I like va - nel - la, You, sa's' - pa - ril - la and I sa's' - pa - rel - la; Va -
G G7 C Am7-5 G C D7 C
ta - to, Pa - tah - to, To - ma - to, To - mah - to!
nil - la, va - nel - la, Choc' - late, straw - b'ry!
Let's Call The Whole Thing

G
C#m7-5
F#7
Bm7
E7-9
Am7
Off! But oh! If we call the whole thing off, Then we must
mf

D9
C#m7-5
F#7
Bm7
E7-9
Am7
part. And oh! If we ev - er part, Then that might break my
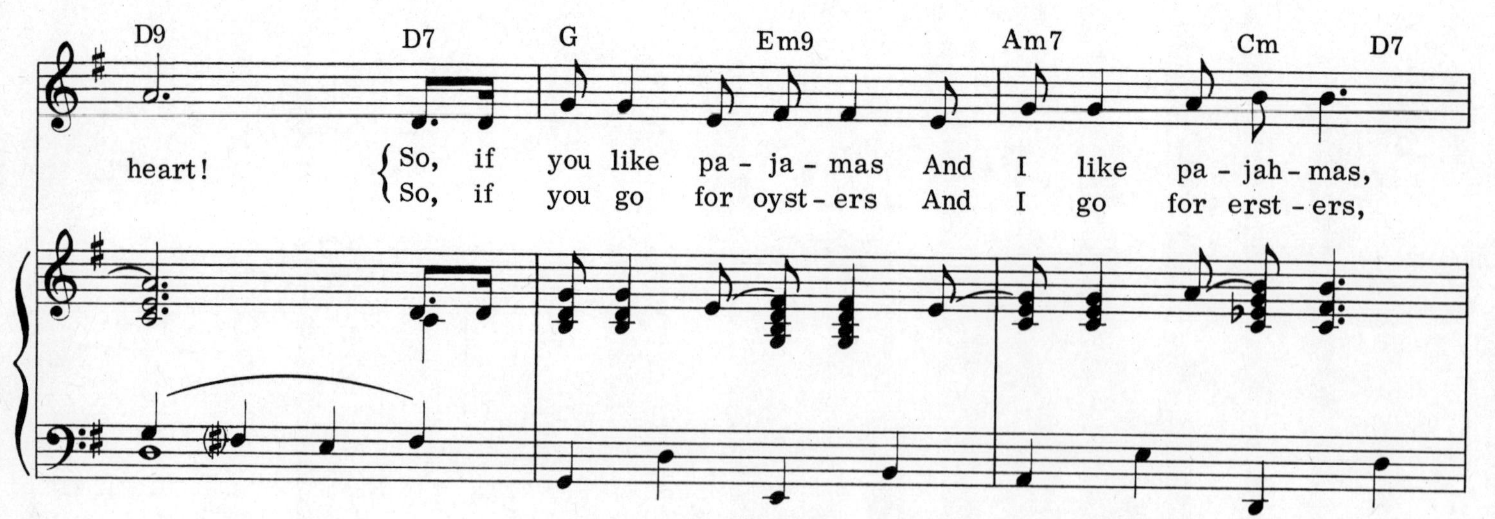
D9
D7
G
Em9
Am7
Cm
D7
heart!
So, if you like pa - ja - mas And I like pa - jah - mas,
So, if you go for oyst - ers And I go for erst - ers,

G
Em9
Am7
Cm
D7
G
G7
I'll wear pa - ja-mas and give up pa -jah-mas.
I'll or - der oyst-ers and can-cel the erst- ers.
For we know we
C
Am7-5
G
C
G
C6
B7+5
B7
E7-9
E7
need each oth - er, So we bet -ter call the call-ing off off.
Am7
Bm
Cmaj7
D7
1.
G
E♭7
D9+5
2.
G
F♯7
G6(9)
Let's Call The Whole Thing Off! Off!

THEY ALL LAUGHED

Lyrics by IRA GERSHWIN

Music by GEORGE GERSHWIN

Am7 Bm Am G D♯dim B+5 B7 Em7
peo - ple from Mis - sou - ri nev - er in - censed me.
Gm6 D Fdim Em7 A7
Oh, I was - n't a bit con - cerned, For from
D Dm Fdim Em7 A7 F♯7 Bm B♭7 D Em7
his - t'ry I had learned How man - y, man - y times the
F♯m A7sus4 A7 D7 D9+5
worm had turned.

Refrain: (happily)
G Em Am D7 Am Cm6 D7
They All Laughed at Chris-to-pher Co-lum-bus When he said the world was round.
They All Laughed at Rock-e-fel-ler Cen-ter Now they're fight-ing to get in.
p-mf
Bm7 Am7 D9+5 G Em Am D7
They All Laughed when Ed-i-son re-cord-ed sound.
They All Laughed at Whit-ney and his cot-ton gin.
G6 Bb A Ab G F# F Em G Em
They All Laughed at
They All Laughed at
3
mf
Am D7 C#7+5 F#9 F#7-9
Wil-bur and his broth-er, When they said that man could fly.
Ful-ton and his steam-boat, Her-shey and his choc-'late bar.

Bm E7 E7+5 D6 D Bm6 A7 A7+5
They told Mar-co-ni Wire-less was a pho-ney;
Ford and his Liz-zie Kept the laugh-ers bus-y;
D9 E9 F9 E9 D9 D Dmaj7 D7 G9 G
It's the same old cry. They laughed at me want-ing
That's how peo-ple are. They laughed at me want-ing
mf
G9 G6 G9 B7+5 E9 E7-9 E7
you, Said I was reach-ing for the moon; But
you, Said it would be Hel-lo, Good-bye; But
A9 A A9 A6 Am C6 E♭7 D9 D
oh, You came through, Now they'll have to change their tune.
oh, You came through, Now they're eat-ing hum-ble pie.

G Em Am D7 B7+5 E7-9
They all said we never could be happy, They laughed at us and
They all said we'd never get together; Darling, let's take a
A9 A7 G E9 Am7 D7
how! But Ho, Ho, Ho! Who's got the last laugh
bow, For, Ho, Ho, Ho! Who's got the last laugh,
1.
G6 A♭dim Adim A♯dim Bdim Cdim D9+5
now?
2.
E♭ B♭ D(Cbass)
He, He, He! Let's at the past laugh,
G E9 Am7 D7 G6(9)
Ha, Ha, Ha! Who's got the last laugh now?
p
mf
f
3

With the Los Angeles Philharmonic (1937).

Ira, portrait by Tommy Amer (1958).

Composer Harold Arlen, Ira and writer Horace Sutton in Russia during the world-wide tour of Porgy and Bess (1956).

THEY CAN'T TAKE THAT AWAY FROM ME

Lyrics by IRA GERSHWIN
Music by GEORGE GERSHWIN

Am7 D7 G6 Am7 D6 Gmaj7 G6 G Am7 D6 D7
mel - o - dy lin-gers on. They may take you from me, I'll miss your fond ca-
Gm Ab C+5 C7 Edim Fm Bb Edim F7 F7-5 Bb7
ress. But though they take you from me, I'll still pos - sess:
poco marcato
Refrain: (slowly, with warmth)
Bb11 Eb6 Ebmaj7 Eb6 Eb Gbdim
The way you wear your hat, The way you sip your tea,
mp-mf
Bb7sus4 Bb7 Fm7 Bb11 Bbm Eb Bb+5
The mem-'ry of all that

Eb9 Cm D7-5 Eb9 Ab Fm7 C9 F7 Bb11
No, no! They Can't Take That A-way From Me! The way your smile just beams
mf
mp
Eb Ebmaj7 Eb6 Eb Gbdim Bb7sus4 Bb7
The way you sing off key,
Fm7 Bb11 Bbm Eb Bb+5 Eb9 Cm D7-5 Eb9
The way you haunt my dreams, No, no! They
mf
Ab Fm7 Bb7sus4 Bb7 Eb6 Eb Gm C9 D7-9
Can't Take That A-way From Me! We may nev-er, nev-er
con calore

Gm C9 D7-9 Gm Em7-5 A7+5 D7sus4 D7
meet a-gain On the bump-y road to love, Still I'll
Gm C9 D7-9 Gm Bbm C7 F7 Abm Bb7
al-ways, al-ways keep the mem-'ry of
mf f
Ab Fm7 Eb6 Ebmaj7 Eb6 Eb Gbdim
The way you hold your knife, The way we danced till three,
mp
Bb7sus4 Bb7 Fm7 Bb11 Eb9 D7-5
The way you've changed my life.

Eb9 Eb11 Eb6 Eb7 Ab Fm7 Bb7sus4 Bb7 Cm Fm7-5
No, no! They Can't Take That A - way From Me! No! They
mf
mp

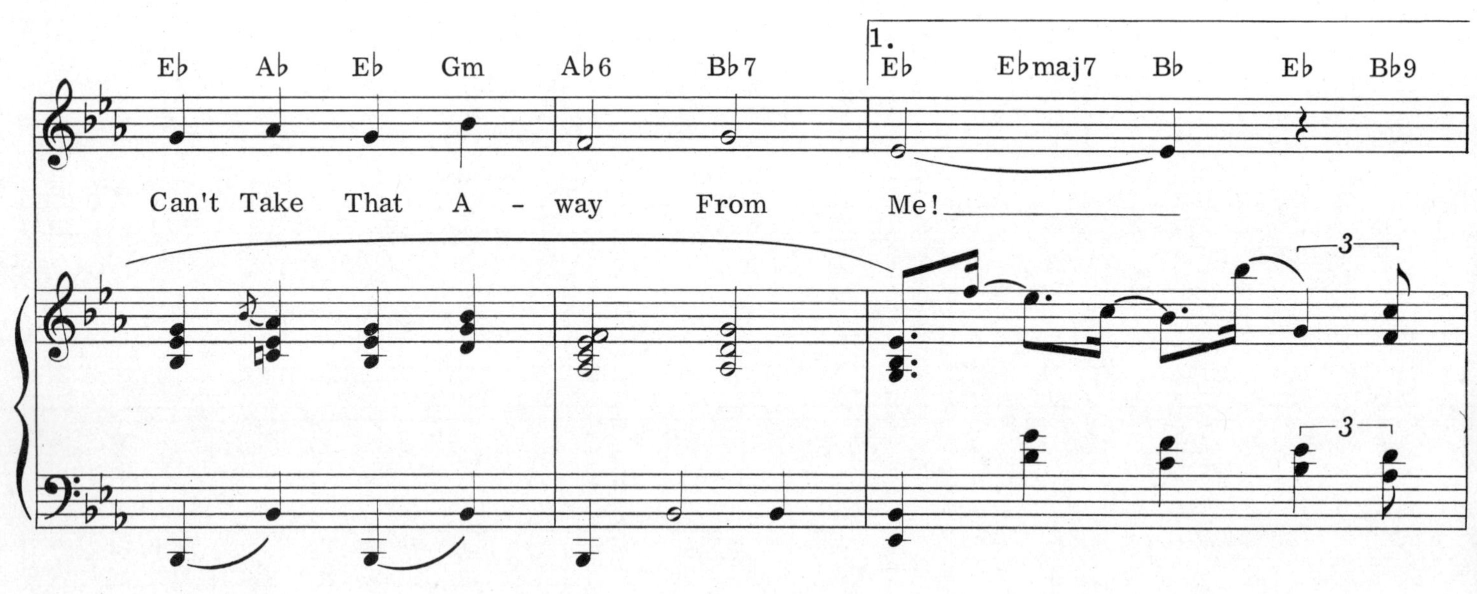
Eb Ab Eb Gm Ab6 Bb7 1. Eb Ebmaj7 Bb Eb Bb9
Can't Take That A - way From Me!
3
3

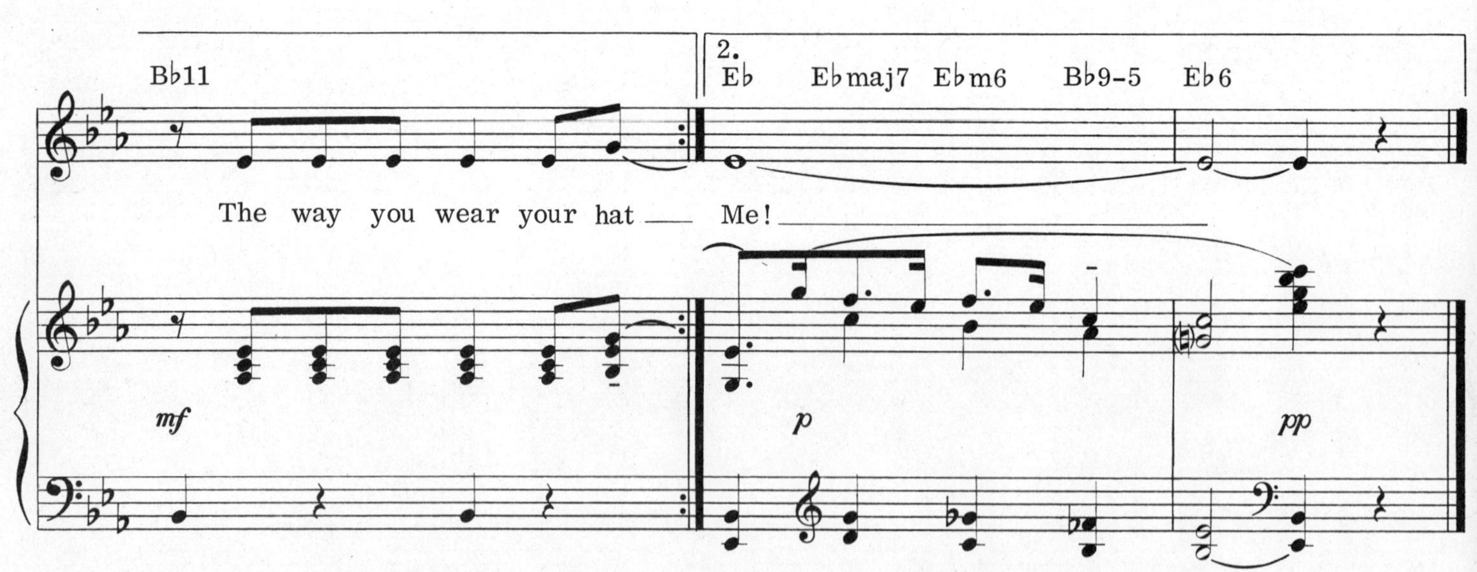
Bb11 2. Eb Ebmaj7 Ebm6 Bb9-5 Eb6
The way you wear your hat Me!
mf
p
pp

A FOGGY DAY

Lyrics by IRA GERSHWIN

Music by GEORGE GERSHWIN

Gm7 C7-9 C7+(-9) Fmaj9 F6 F Am Am6 Am7 D9 D7-9
out-look was de-cid-ed-ly blue. But as I walked through the fog-gy streets a-lone, It
Am Adim Gm7 C7 F C11 F
turned out to be the luck-iest day I've known.
Refrain:
(brighter but warmly)
C7 F Ebm6 Gm7 C9
A Fog-gy Day in Lon-don town
p
C7-9 F Fm7 Dm7-5 G7(6) G7+ C9
Had me low and had me down.

Fmaj7 Fmaj7(-5) E7-5 F9 Bbmaj7 Bbm6
I viewed the morn-ing with a - larm,
mp
Fmaj7 D9 G9(6) G9+5 C9
The Brit - ish Mu - se - um had lost its charm.
C7 F Ebm6 Gm7 C9
How long, I won - dered, could this thing last?
p
C7-9 F Fm7 Dm7-5 G7(6) G7+5 C9
But the age of mir - a - cles had - n't passed,

F11 F9(6) F7(-9) B♭maj7 G9-5
For, sud - den - ly, I saw you there,
mf
Dm B♭m6 F B♭6 Fmaj7 B♭6 Dm7 G9
And through fog - gy Lon - don town the sun was shin - ing
p
1. Gm7 C7 F Fmaj7 C7 F7 B♭7 B♭m6 D♭+5 C7
ev - 'ry - where. A
mf
2. F Fmaj7 C7 F7 B♭7 B♭m6 Dm6 B♭m6 Fmaj7
- where.
8va
mf
dim.
pp

NICE WORK IF YOU CAN GET IT

Lyrics by IRA GERSHWIN

Music by GEORGE GERSHWIN

D Fdim Em7 A7 D9
There's no guar - an - tee that time won't e-rase his name.
D9+5 D7+5 G Em7 Em6 Am7 D7
The fact is, the on - ly work that real - ly brings en - joy-ment
G G(F♯bass) Em6 F♯7 Bm Bm7 Bdim Em6
Is the kind that is for girl and boy meant, Fall in love you won't re - gret it,
Bm E7-9 Am9 Cm6 D7 G6 Am6
That's the best work of all if you can get it.

Refrain: (smoothly)
B7+5
E9
A7+5
D9
G7
C9
A9
A7-9
Hold-ing hands at mid-night 'Neath a star-ry sky,
p - mf
G
G6
Am7
G
C6
G Edim D11
G
Nice Work If You Can Get It, And you can get it if you try.
B7+5
E9
A7+5
D9
G7
C9
A9
A7-9
Strol-ling with the one girl, Sigh-ing sigh af-ter sigh,

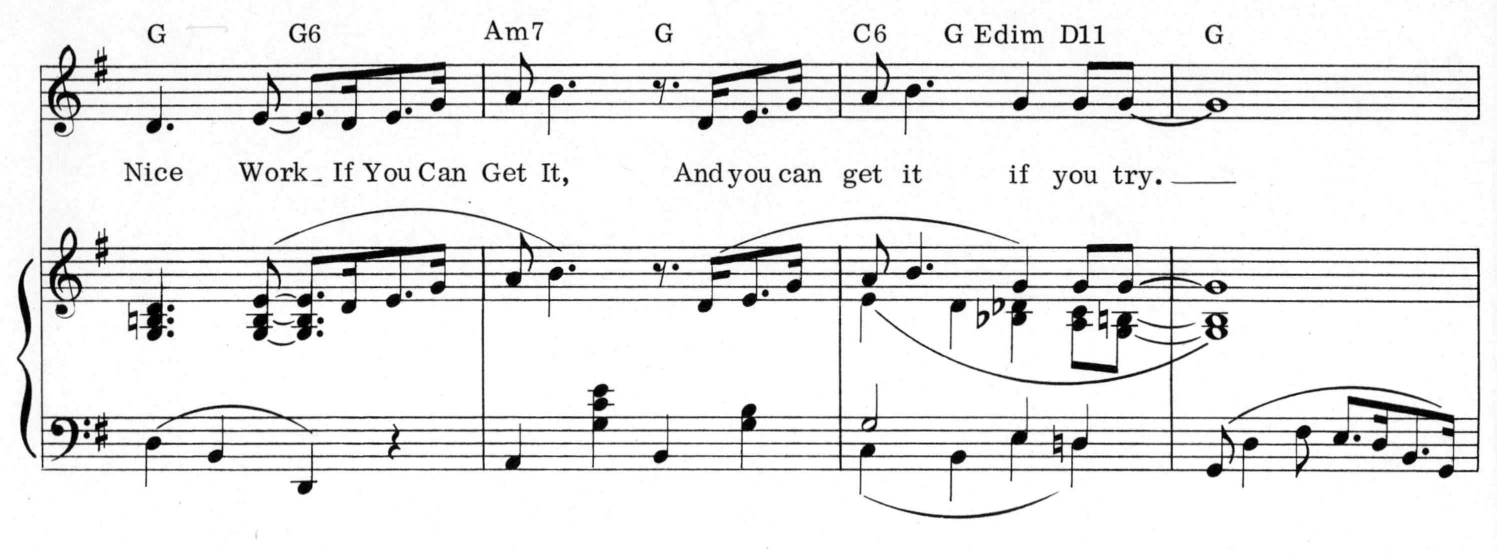
G G6 Am7 G C6 G Edim D11 G
Nice Work_ If You Can Get It, And you can get it if you try.

Em C9+11 C9 Em Em7 A9
Just im-ag - ine some - one Wait - ing at the cot - tage door,
mp

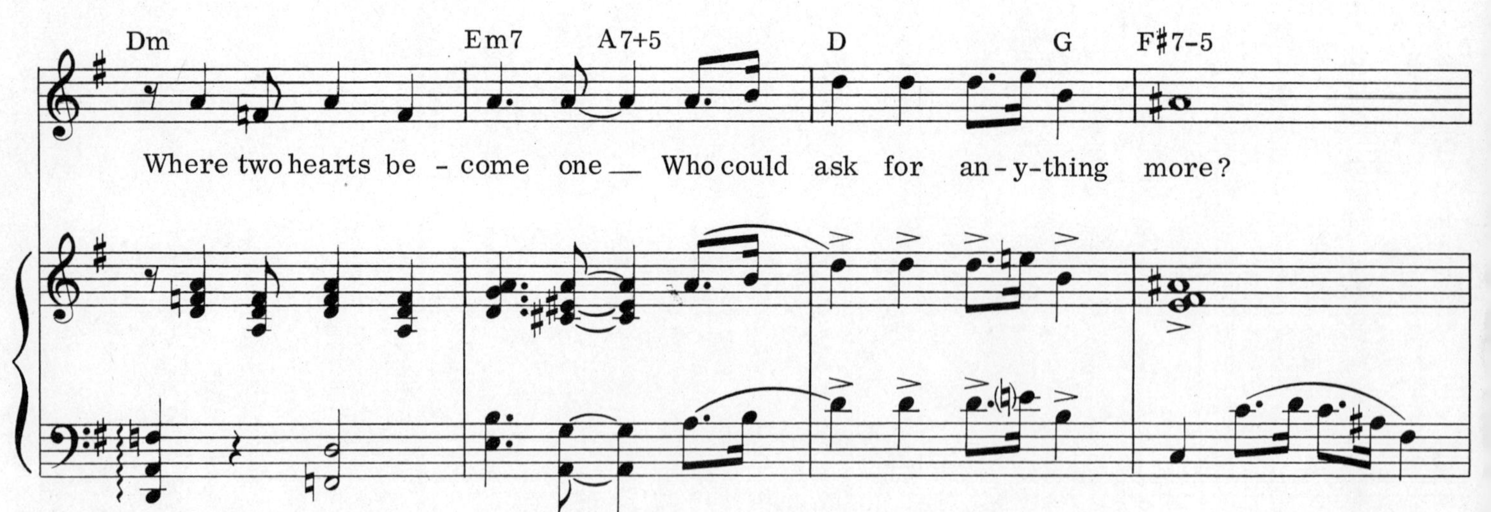
Dm Em7 A7+5 D G F♯7-5
Where two hearts be - come one Who could ask for an - y - thing more?

B7+5
E9
A7+5
D9
G7
C9
A9
A7-9
Lov - ing one who loves you, And then tak - ing that vow,
G
G6
Am7
G
F7-5
E7
Am9
D11
C7
Nice Work If You Can Get It, And if you get it, Won't you tell me
G
Em7
Am6
C+5
how?
G
F+5
Eb7
D7+5
G6/9
how?

LOVE IS HERE TO STAY

Lyrics by IRA GERSHWIN | Music by GEORGE GERSHWIN

Am7 F G7(6) C9 C7 B♭maj7 Am7 Gm7 Fmaj7
last - ing, But that is - n't our af - fair; We've got some-thing
Em7-5 A7 D D6 G9 C9 C9-5 Gm C9
per-ma-nent, I mean in the way we care.
Refrain:
C7 B♭ C♯dim G9 Gm7 C7 F6 F
It's ver - y clear Our Love Is Here To Stay;
p - mf
Gm7 C7 G7(6) C11 C7 E♭9 D9
Not for a year, But ev - er and a day.

G9 B♭7-5 G7 C7 D7+5 Gm7 C7(6)
The ra - di - o and the tel - e - phone and the
Fmaj9 B♭maj9 B♭6 Em7-5 A7+5 A7 Dm
mov - ies that we know May just be pass - ing fan - cies,
G7 F♯7 G7 Gm7 C7 B♭ C♯dim G9
And in time may go. But, oh my dear,
mf
p
Gm7 C7 F6 F Gm7 C7
Our Love Is Here To Stay; To - geth - er

G7(6) C11 C7 E♭9 D9
we're go - ing a long, long way.
G9 B♭7-5 G7 C7 D7+5 Gm7 C7(6)
In time the Rock - ies may crum - ble, Gi - bral - tar may tum - ble,
E♭9 D9 D7+5 -9 B♭6 Ddim Fmaj7 F6 Fmaj7 Gm11 C9
They're on - ly made of clay, But Our Love Is Here To
8va
mp
dim.
1. F6 C9(6) C7 B♭ C♯dim
Stay. It's ver - y
2. F6 C9(6) F6(9)
Stay.
p
mf
pp delicato
pp
Ped

LOVE WALKED IN

Lyrics by IRA GERSHWIN

Music by GEORGE GERSHWIN

Bbm7 Eb7 Abmaj9 Ab6 Am7 D7 Gmaj7 Bb9
Time was stand - ing still, No one count - ed till There
Eb Ebmaj7 Edim Fm7 Db7-5 F7 Bb7 Eb Fm7 Bb9 Bb9+5
came a knock - knock - knock - ing at the door.
Refrain: slowly, with much expression
Eb F7
Love walked right in and drove the shad - ows a -
p
Bb7(sus4) Bb7 Eb F7
way; Love walked right in and brought my sun - ni - est

Bb7
Eb
Eb+5
Ab
Ab6
day.
One
ma - gic mo - ment and my heart seemed to
mf
C7+5
Fm
C7
Fm7
Eb
Ab
Eb
know
That love said "Hel - lo,"
Though not a
mp
F9
Fm7
Bb7
Eb
word was spo - ken.
One
look and I for -
poco rit.
p a tempo
F7
Bb7(sus4)
Bb7
Eb
got the gloom of the past;
One

F7 Bb7
look and I had found my fu - ture at last.
Eb Eb+5 Ab
One look and I had found a
mf
Fm7 Abm6 Eb Eb7 C7 Fm Bb7
world com - plete - ly new, When Love Walked In with
dim.
1. Eb B9 Bb7
you.
p
2. Eb Gb Bb9 Eb
you.
p
pp
Ped. *

THE BACK BAY POLKA

Lyrics by IRA GERSHWIN

Music by GEORGE GERSHWIN

C
G7
C
G7
Think as your neigh-bors think, Make lem - on - ade your drink;
Keep up the cul - tured pose, Keep look - ing down your nose,
One day it's much too hot, Then cold as you know what,
No song ex - cept a hymn, And keep your lan- guage prim;
C
Am
D7
C
G7
C
You'll be the Miss - ing Link If you don't wear spats in Bos - ton.
Keep up the stat - us quos Or they keep you out of Bos - ton.
In all the world there's not weath-er an - y - where like Bos - ton.
You call a leg a limb, Or they boot you out of Bos - ton.
Em
A7
Em
A7
Paint - ers who paint the nude We keep re - press-ing;
Books that are out of key We quick-ly bur - y.
At nat - 'ral his - to - ry We are co - los - sal.
You're of the bour-geoi - sie And no one both- ers,
mp

Dm Am B7 G9+5
We take the at - ti - tude E - ven a sal - ad must have dress-ing.
You will find lib - er - ty In Mis-ter Web-ster's dic - tion - a - ry.
That is be - cause, you see, At first hand we stud - y the fos - sil.
Not if your fam-'ly tree Does-n't date from the Pil-grim Fa-thers.
C G7 C
New York or Phil - a - delph' Won't put you
Laugh - ter goes up the flue. Life is one
Strang - ers are all dis - missed. Not that we're
There - fore when all is said, Life is so
mp
G7 C Am D7
on the shelf If you would be your - self, But you
big ta - boo. No mat - ter what you do, It
pre - ju - diced, You sim - ply don't ex - ist If you
lim - it - ed, You find, un - less you're dead, You

C G7 C Am6
can't be your-self in Bos - ton. You can't be your-self, You
is - n't be - ing done in Bos - ton. It is - n't be - ing done, It
have - n't been born in Bos - ton. You have - n't been born, You
nev - er get a - head in Bos - ton. You nev - er get a - head Un -
G7 A7 Dm7 G7 C
can't be your-self, You can't be your-self in Bos - ton!
is - n't be - ing done, It is - n't be - ing done in Bos - ton!
have - n't been born, If you have - n't been born in Bos - ton!
less you're dead, You nev - er get a - head in Bos - ton!
Optional Interlude
C G7 C7 G7
f
C7 F Ab7 G7 C

FOR YOU, FOR ME, FOR EVERMORE

Lyrics by IRA GERSHWIN

Music by GEORGE GERSHWIN

Cm F9 Bb11 Bb7 Eb Ebdim Fm7 Bb9
If we walk on air. All the shad-ows now will lose us,
Eb11 Eb7 Ab6 G7 Cm G+5 Cm7
Luck-y stars are ev-'ry-where. As a hap-py
F9 Fm7 Bb9
be-ing, Here's what I'm for-see-ing:
poco rit.
Chorus: (not fast)
Bb7 Eb F7 Bb11 Bb7 Fm7 Bb7
For You, For Me, For Ev-er-more, It's
p-mf

E♭ F7 B♭11 B♭7 Fm7 B♭7
bound to be for ev - er - more. It's
B♭m9 B♭m7 E♭7 B♭m9 E♭9
plain to see, we found by find - ing each
A♭maj9 A♭6 A♭ Cm9 Cm7 F7 B7
oth - er, The love we wait - ed for.
B♭7+5 B♭7 E♭ F7 B♭11 B♭7
I'm yours, you're mine, and in our hearts
mp

Fm7 Bb7 Bbm9 Bbm7 Eb7 Abadd9 Ab
The hap - py end - ing starts.
G7+5(Fbass) Fm7-5 Eb(Bbbass) Gm Fm7 Bb7
What a love - ly world this world will be, With a
Eb Bb Cm7 F9 F7 Fm7 Eb Fm7 Bb7
world of love in store For You, For Me, For Ev - er -
1. Eb6 Cm6 Bb7
More! For
2. Eb6 Eb
More.
mf

GERSHWIN AT THE KEYBOARD
ARRANGED BY THE COMPOSER

America, in the last twenty years, has become a veritable hotbed of popular music. During this fruitful period it has mothered some of the best music to be found in the musical comedy of the time. The way had been prepared, of course, as long ago as the epoch before the Civil War, when the minstrel show was in its palmy days and we already had truly popular songs and popular composers, not to speak of the faint beginnings of jazz bands and Tin Pan Alley methods long before the pavement of Tin Pan Alley was laid.

American popular music, since its origin, has been steadily gaining in originality; today it may truly lay claim to being the most vital of contemporary popular music. Unfortunately, however, most songs die at an early age and are soon completely forgotten by the self-same public that once sang them with such gusto. The reason for this is that they are sung and played too much when they are alive, and cannot stand the strain of their very popularity. This is especially true since the invention of the phonograph, and more so since the wide-spread conquest of the air waves.

When the publishers asked me to gather a group of my songs for publication I took up the idea enthusiastically, because I thought that this might be a means of prolonging their life. It also occurred to me that the idea might be taken up by other composers of popular music.

Sheet music, as ordinarily printed for mass sales, is arranged with an eye to simplicity. The publishers cannot be blamed for getting out simplified versions of songs, since the majority of the purchasers of popular music are little girls with little hands, who have not progressed very far in their study of the piano. At that, if you have the patience to compare the arrangements of our old-time popular music with those of our latter-day hits, the latter-day arrangements, simple as they are, will appear complicated by contrast.

Gradually, with the general increase of technical skill at the piano, there has arisen a demand for arrangements that shall consider that skill. Playing my songs as frequently as I do at private parties, I have naturally been led to compose numerous variations upon them, and to indulge the desire for complication and variety that every composer feels when he manipulates the same material over and over again. It was this habit of mine that led to the original suggestion to publish a group of songs not only in the simplified arrangements that the public knew, but also in the variations that I had devised.

Hence, in this book, the transcriptions for solo piano of each chorus, after its appearance in the regular sheet-music form. Some of these are very difficult; they have been put in for those good pianists, of whom there is a growing number, who enjoy popular music but who rebel at the too-simple arrangements issued by the publishers with the average pianist in view.

In a country that spends so much money on its dance music it was inevitable that there should be a radical development in the playing of its most important instrument—the piano. The evolution of our popular pianistic style really began with the introduction of ragtime, just before Spanish-American War, and came to its culminating point in the jazz era that followed upon the Great War. A number of names come crowding into my memory; Mike Bernard, Les Copeland, Melville Ellis, Lucky Roberts, Zez Confrey, Arden and Ohman, and others. Each of these was responsible for the popularization of a new technique, or a new wrinkle in playing. Some of my readers will recall various of these procedures, of which a number were really but stunts. There was the habit of Les Copeland had of thumping his left hand onto a blurred group of notes, from which he would slide into a regular chord; it made a rather interesting pulse in the bass, a sort of happy-go-lucky *sforzando* effect. Then there was Bernard's habit of playing the melody in the left hand, while he wove a filigree of counterpoint with the right; for a time this was all the rage, as it sounded pretty well to ears that were not accustomed to the higher musical processes. Confrey's contribution has been of a more permanent nature, as some of his piano figures found their way into serious American composition.

To all of these predecessors I am indebted; some of the effects I use in my transcriptions derive from their style of playing the piano.

Now, the American piano player of popular songs has managed to keep pace with the progress of the song that he plays. As the American popular song has grown richer in harmony and rhythm, so has the player grown more subtle and incisive in his performance of it.

One chief hint as to the style best adapted in performance of these pieces is in order. To play American popular music most effectively one must guard against the natural tendency to make too frequent use of the sustaining pedal. Our study of the great romantic composers has trained us in the method of the *legato,* whereas our popular music asks for *staccato* effects, for almost a stencilled style. The rhythms of American popular music are more or less brittle; they should be made to snap, and at times to cackle. The more sharply the music is played, the more effective it sounds.

Most pianists with a classical training fail lamentably in the playing of our ragtime or jazz because they use the pedaling of Chopin when interpreting the blues of Handy. The romantic touch is very good in a sentimental ballad, but in a tune of strict rhythm it is somewhat out of place.

I wish to thank B. G. De Sylva, Irving Caesar, Ballard MacDonald, Gus Kahn, and my brother, Ira Gershwin and many others for their valued assistance.

Spring, 1932 George Gershwin

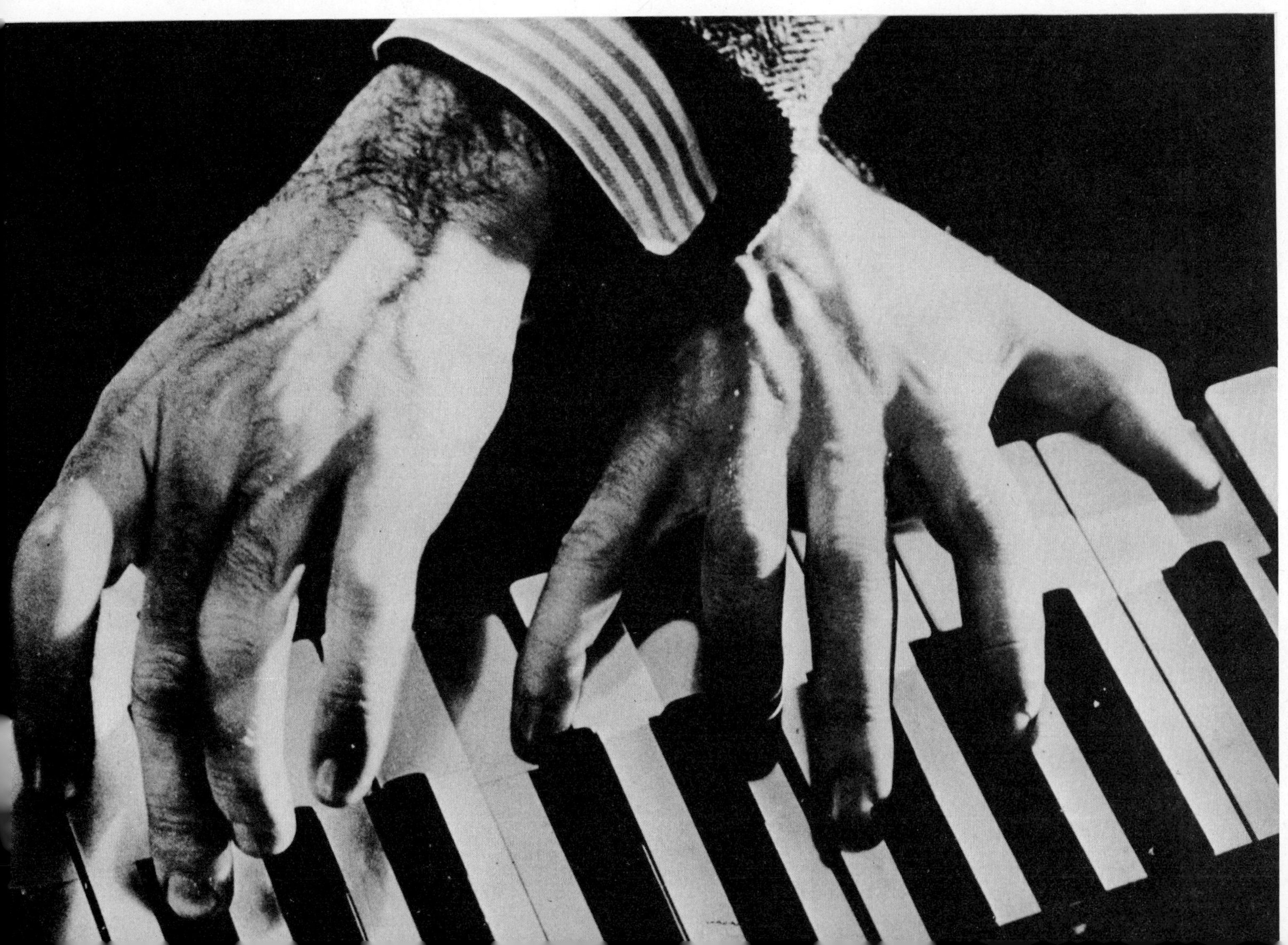

THE MAN I LOVE

Lyrics by IRA GERSHWIN

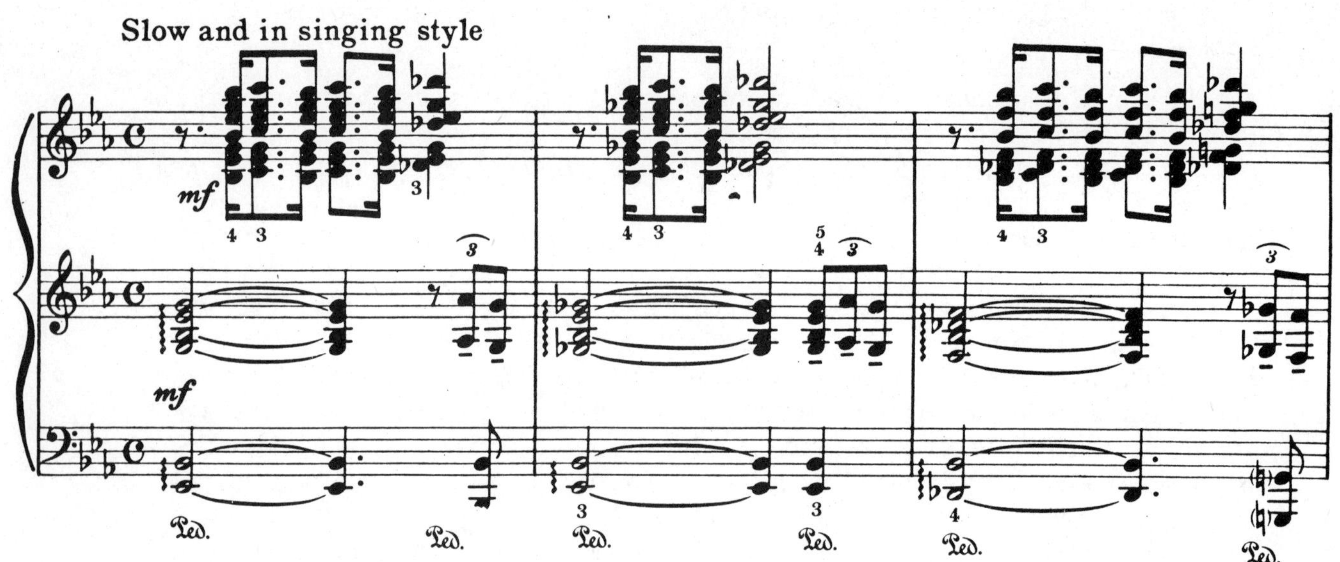

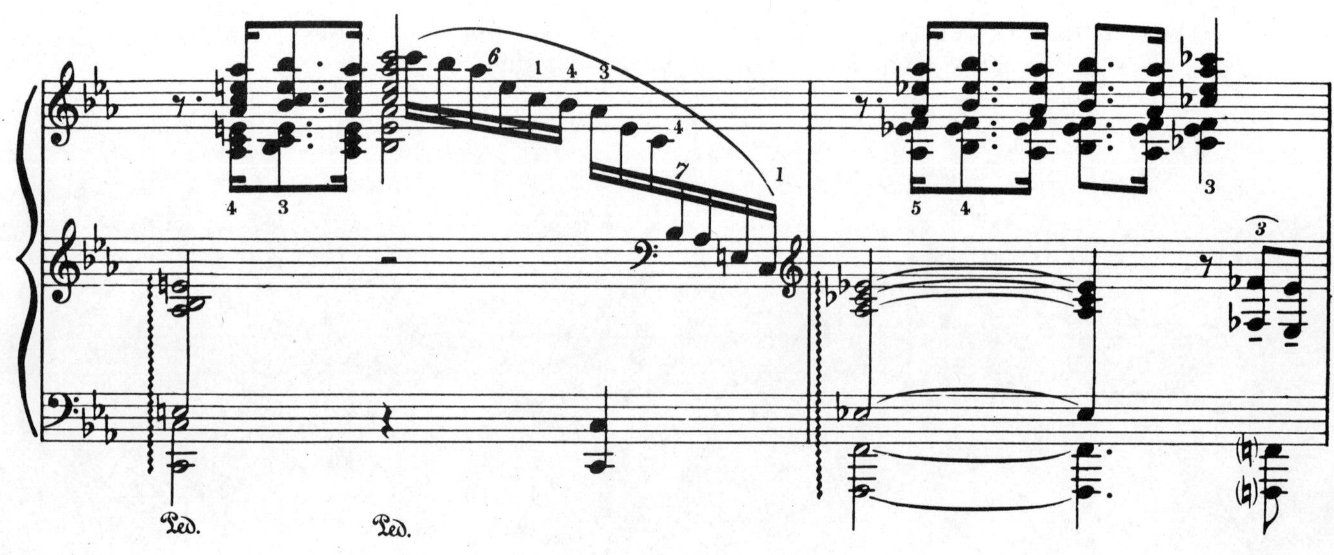

R.H.
L.H.
marcato
rit.
a tempo
legato
p

mf
mf
un poco rit.
a tempo
p
dim.
p
R.H.
L.H.
Ped.

SWANEE

Lyrics by IRVING CAESAR

mf
molto cresc.
f
decresc.
mf
p
Ped.
pp

NOBODY BUT YOU

Lyrics by B. G. DeSYLVA

mf
L.H.
L.H.
dim.
Ped.

I'LL BUILD A STAIRWAY TO PARADISE

Lyrics by B. G. DeSYLVA &
ARTHUR FRANCIS (Ira Gershwin)

p
f
R.H.
L.H.
p
rit.

DO IT AGAIN

Lyrics by B. G. DeSYLVA

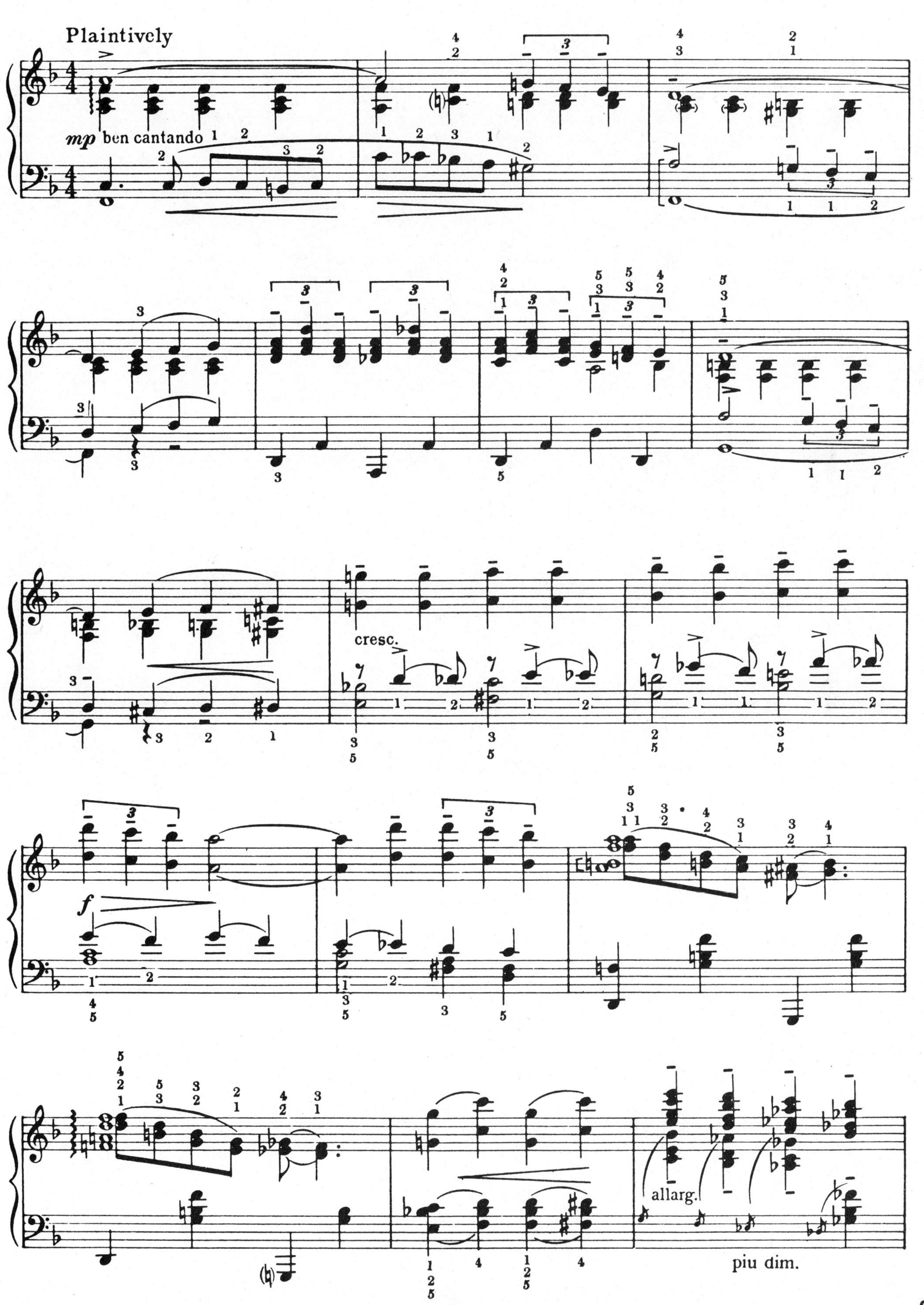

mp
legato
a tempo
pp
pp
delicatiss.
cresc
R.H.
p subito
mf
p
dim.
Ped. Ped.

FASCINATING RHYTHM

humoroso
sf
mf
L.H.
mp
dim.
p
rit.
Presto
L.H.
R.H.
L.H.

OH, LADY BE GOOD

Lyrics by IRA GERSHWIN

ff
il basso marcato
p
poco a poco cresc.
f

SOMEBODY LOVES ME

Lyrics by BALLARD MACDONALD & B.G. DeSYLVA

p
f
mf
mf
mf
Ped.

SWEET AND LOW-DOWN

Lyrics by IRA GERSHWIN

marcato
mp
f

CLAP YO' HANDS

Lyrics by IRA GERSHWIN

DO-DO-DO

Lyrics by IRA GERSHWIN

playfully

MY ONE AND ONLY

Lyrics by IRA GERSHWIN

broadly
f
mp staccato
f
mp staccato
mf
p
sfz
mf
p

'S WONDERFUL

Lyrics by IRA GERSHWIN

Ped.
Ped.
decresc.
gliss.
L.H.
rit. e dim.

STRIKE UP THE BAND

Lyrics by IRA GERSHWIN

piquantly
Ped.

I GOT RHYTHM

Lyrics by IRA GERSHWIN

R.H.
Ped.

f
p
mf

cresc.
Martellato
R.H.

WHO CARES?

Lyrics by IRA GERSHWIN

L. H.
melody ben marcato

THAT CERTAIN FEELING

Lyrics by IRA GERSHWIN

cresc.
decresc.
f
sf p

LIZA

Lyrics by IRA GERSHWIN & GUS KAHN

legato
mf
marcato
simile
poco a poco cresc.
Ped.
Ped.
Ped.
f
L.H.
mf

Very marked
poco a poco cresc.
R.H.
L.H.
dim.
poco a poco cresc.
R.H.

sf
sf
sf
sf
Ped.
Ped.
Ped.
Ped.
L.H.
mf
Ped.
❊
marcato
legato
mp
Ped.
Ped.
Ped.
Ped.
Ped.
Ped.
Ped.
Ped.
Ped.
Ped.

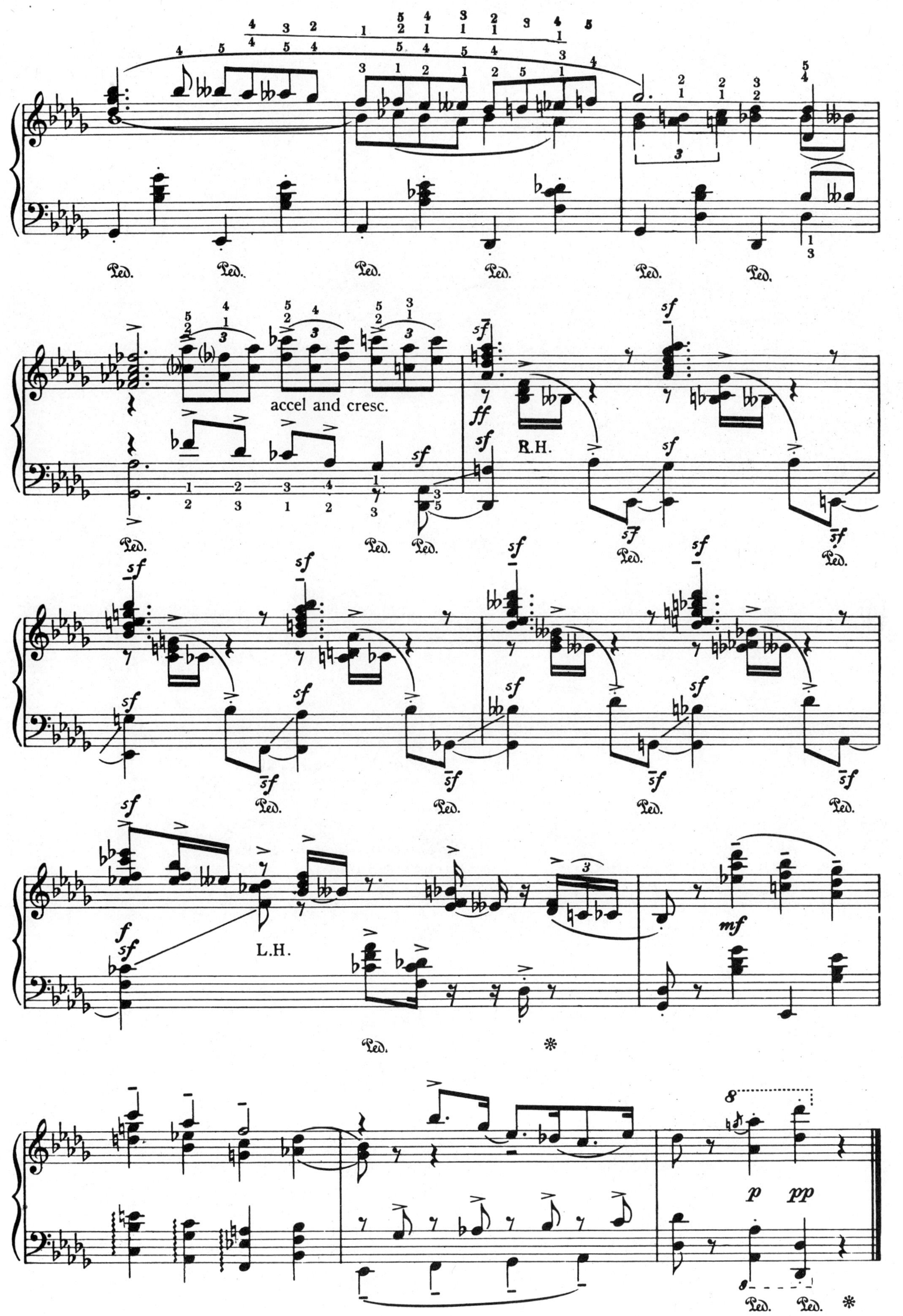
accel and cresc.
R.H.
L.H.

ALPHABETICAL INDEX OF SONGS

A Foggy Day, 254
An American In Paris, 103
The Babbitt And The Bromide, 94
The Back Bay Polka, 271
Bess, You Is My Woman Now, 211
Bidin' My Time, 119
Blah-Blah-Blah, 135
Blue Blue Blue, 191
But Not For Me, 131
By Strauss, 232
Clap Yo' Hands, 62
Concerto In F, 56
Cuban Overture, 163
Delishious, 139
Do-Do-Do, 67
Embraceable You, 123
Fascinating Rhythm, 27
For You, For Me, For Evermore, 275
Funny Face, 77
Gershwin At The Keyboard, 279
He Loves And She Loves, 85
I Got Plenty O' Nuttin', 204
I Got Rhythm, 127
I Loves You Porgy, 225
I'll Build A Stairway to Paradise, 19
Isn't It A Pity? 169
It Ain't Necessarily So, 219
I've Got A Crush On You, 99
Let 'Em Eat Cake, 185
Let's Call The Whole Thing Off, 237
Liza, 105
Looking For A Boy, 43
Lorelei, 164
Love Is Here To Stay, 263
Love Is Sweeping The Country, 153
Love Walked In, 267
The Man I Love, 36
Maybe, 58
Mine, 179
Mischa, Yascha, Toscha, Sascha, 15
My Cousin In Milwaukee, 174
My Man's Gone Now, 198
My One And Only, 89
Nice Work If You Can Get It, 258
Of Thee I Sing, 149
Oh, Lady Be Good, 33
Preludes For Piano, 76
The Real American Folk Song (Is A Rag), 3
Rhapsody In Blue, 41
'S Wonderful, 81
Second Rhapsody, 161
Somebody Loves Me, 23
Someone To Watch Over Me, 71
Soon, 109
Strike Up The Band, 113
Summertime, 194
Swanee, 9
Sweet And Low-Down, 51
That Certain Feeling, 47
They All Laughed, 243
They Can't Take That Away From Me, 249
Wintergreen For President, 144
Who Cares?, 157

73 74 75 5 4 3 2 1